To Dave & Family – Hope you enjoy! ☺

PIONEER PADDLING COLONIAL CAROLINA

By William D. Auman

William D.
Auman

First published by Dog Ear Publishing
4010 W. 86th Street, Ste H
Indianapolis, IN 46268
www.dogearpublishing.net

dog ear
PUBLISHING

ISBN: 978-160844-526-4

This book is printed on acid-free paper.

Printed in the United States of America

To the Lizard, Coach "D", and the Munchkin

TABLE OF CONTENTS

PROLOGUE

Many of you who will read this book already belong to the world of the less-traveled, or should I say that realm of the imagination that can lead to all kinds of surreal experiences. Hang on...the reality is out there. We just have to look for it. It can be found around the corner, on the other side, or in the middle. It's all in the perspective. No, this is not a book about eastern religion, nor was it written by a loosely-associated mystic. It is, however, about the canoe and kayak experiences of a somewhat abnormal paddling fanatic who would like to share some information and perspectives that have accumulated over the past 35+ years on the water.

This is not designed to be just another guidebook for the thrill-seeking extremist, but rather will maintain a particular degree of focus on family-oriented "wilderness" experiences presented within the historical context through which they unfold. As my wife and I have discovered, some of the most enjoyable times of one's life can be had when accompanied by the inquiring minds of young children. Ours began their paddling careers at ages 3 and 2 respectively, and have continued to offer inspiration and insight when we are fortunate enough to have them along. Whereas most outfitters tend to cater to the wild water enthusiasts and backcountry solitude seekers, there are many exciting and non-technical day trips out there to be explored by even the most novice of paddlers. Only a few strokes of the paddle can take you and yours back to a simpler time.

Enough of the monologue, and on to the message. In this book you could assume the role of John Lawson, the infamous English explorer and historian who set sail to the Carolinas in August of 1700 to assume appointment as Surveyor-General of North Carolina. At that time the Carolina swamps and backcountry were essentially unknown and forbidding destinations, but remnants of those habitats can still be encountered today. You may choose to frequent the haunts of the legendary pirate Edward Teach (aka **Blackbeard**) along our majestic seaboard, and paddle in the wake of the *Queen Anne's Revenge* near Beaufort.

Perhaps you will decide to continue your path across the state and nurture your appreciation for the abundance of colonial wilderness that still exists in the coastal plain. Some of the most pristine creeks and blackwater streams, many with ties to historical events of the pioneer era, flow throughout the region and are quite accessible for any paddler. Even the Piedmont, with its bustling population and municipalities, has a call to water complete with some sense of wilderness escape tucked here and there in the nooks and crannies. With most of those areas being located on a regional edge, some technically "piedmont paddles" will be found in both sections two and three of the book. Finally, no adventure would be complete without mention of the author's adopted home, our Appalachian "Land of Sky." Both moderate whitewater and crystal clear mountain lakes with mirrored clouds await those who desire the ultimate in serenity that paddling has to offer.

During the progression of the project at hand (that being to finish this book that has been a work in progress since the 1980s), I have attempted to narrow the countless bodies of water in our Old North State into which my paddle has dipped down to a chosen number that stand out in their own special way. North Carolina is home to bountiful paddling options, hence the "chosen number" easily surpasses 100. The result is designed to provide a broad base of varied opportunities for the readers to choose from when creating their own experiences, although not rising to the level of being a fully comprehensive guidebook.

North Carolina's familiar "from the mountains to the sea" slogan has essentially been reversed in this setting, since we begin with a visit to the eastern seaboard and work our way west. In each section of the book I will attempt to provide pertinent paddling information within a historical framework that will hopefully serve to enhance your time on the water, and the magical memories that will permeate your thoughts upon return. Every trip, even our habitual backyard route along the French Broad River, maintains a degree of uniqueness all its own. The art of paddling, subject to the varying conditions supplied by wind, waves, and rapids, is the equivalent of poetry in motion. The imprint, while individual, presents a universal message that will remain with you and yours as time goes by.

The beauty of the paddling experience is that you, as Robert Frost described many years ago, have chosen to take the path less traveled by, and it *will* make all the difference. That "difference" can take on many forms. You may choose to take along your young son or daughter and decide to go island-hopping in search of those magic dragons or hobbits that might just still be out there. En route you can thrill to the sight of the flying pterosaur, known in the modern era as the great blue heron, as it follows the celestial horizon. Certainly, other dinosaurs can be found just around the next bend in the river, if not their descendants.

Why not integrate that sense of imagination with elements of inner peace and solitude as you venture out into the early morning fog at a time when the natural world around you is beginning to awaken. Then again, you may prefer the brilliant hues of the sunset as it reflects a spectrum of rainbow across the rippling water. When you close your eyes for a moment you may lose track of time, and envision the harmony of being at one with your surroundings just as life was meant to be. The late Sigurd Olson, in his book *The Singing Wilderness*, perhaps best describes the experience:

"The movement of a canoe is like a reed in the wind...it is part of the medium through which it flows, the sky, the water, the shores...A man is part of his canoe and therefore part of all he knows. The instant he dips a paddle, he flows as it flows...moving across a calm surface with mirrored clouds...the sensation of suspension between heaven and earth, of paddling not on the water but through the skies themselves."

There is a brother/sisterhood that attaches to those who seek it. I hope this book will assist you on that journey. As a practical matter, I also hope you will find it to be an educational tool that will simply add to your family or individual enjoyment of North Carolina's remaining wilderness waterways...from the sea to the mountains.

Springer's Point, Ocracoke Island.
The site of Blackbeard's final beach blast

Chapter One:

In Search of Blackbeard's Ghost

"Only the devil and I know the whereabouts of my treasure, and the one of us who lives the longest should take it all"

—*Edward Teach*

The coastal region of the Old North State is rich in history and laden with golden opportunities to paddle into Neverland, even if you only have a few hours to get away. The English conquest of the seaboard begins with the Fort Raleigh expedition, which later set the stage for the Lost Colony. John White and company encountered Native Americans (generally thought to be part of the Algonquian nation which today is centrally located in Ontario) paddling what is now the Roanoke Sound in their cypress dugout canoes. Some of the first tribes to interact with the colonists included the Pasquotank, Chowan, Pamlico, Tuscarora and Roanoke. These names resonate in contemporary society as designations for cities, counties, rivers, lakes and sounds. One of the most beautiful islands in the world holds claim to a tribal namesake of Algonquian origin, that being Ocracoke. It is designated on an early map drawn by John White in 1585 as *Woccocock*, and sometimes appears on other maps as being *Wocon*, or *Wokokin*.

A popular local story attributes the name to the pirate Blackbeard from the year 1718. The impatient pirate captain walked the deck of his ship all night while waiting for the onset signal of what was to become the Battle of Ocracoke Inlet. He knew that when the cock first crowed, the action would begin, and suddenly cried out "O Crow Cock!" several times. Had he known that this morning of battle would be his last, perhaps he would have not been so inclined to rush the issue! Pirates were actually the first Europeans to frequent the Outer Banks, including Ocracoke, so perhaps it is befitting to begin our paddling zone at this locale in the center of the majestic Carolina coast.

A. Ocracoke to Beaufort and the Pamlico

I doubt that Captain Edward Teach (aka Edward Thatch, aka Blackbeard), had any idea that the morning of November 22, 1718, would end with his severed head being strapped to the bow pulpit of the invading sloop of

Virginia's Lt. Maynard. Accordingly, he probably did not name the island of Ocracoke. In fact, he and his remaining crew on the *Adventure,* the ship of which he received vested title from the vice-admiralty court in Bath, were probably quite hung over from their final beach blast of grog at Springer's Point the night before. Maynard had been sent by Governor Spotswood of Virginia, uninvited, to encroach upon colonial Carolina and kill the pirate, who had recently received a pardon from his part-time neighbor, Governor Eden of North Carolina. To make a long story short, Blackbeard succumbed to his assassins from the Royal Navy in hand to hand combat after being shot a total of five times and stabbed at least twenty. His headless body supposedly swam around Maynard's sloop three times before sinking into Teach's Hole.

Teach's Hole is the local name for the sound side of the southern tip of Ocracoke Island, just off Springer's Point, which is the highest point on the island and marked by its rocky shoreline. Legend has it that the pirate crew enjoyed quite a party at that venue during the evening prior to Maynard's attack. After taking the ferry from either Cedar Island (see below), Swan Quarter, or Hatteras (the free one), put your canoe or kayak into Silver Lake Harbor and turn left as you paddle through the "Ditch" just next to the National Park Service Visitor Center. In less than a mile you will see the point and sandy beach, which is a great spot for a picnic lunch or bottle of rum if you are feeling pyrated. Take time to scan the trails, which are well marked, and perhaps a glint in the sand will reveal a piece of eight or doubloon (note that modern era pirates have been known to leave replica coins at the site to enhance the thrill of the young explorer who makes the trek). While en route towards the point, keep a look out for the blue crab and manta rays that appear in the clear waters that surround the island. You don't need a glass bottom boat to see them, although finding the *Adventure* may be slightly more difficult. People consider it to perhaps be Blackbeard's "sugar ship", and pirate treasure may well have been buried with it under the ocean floor. Good luck.

The flagship of the pirate, the forty cannon *Queen Anne's Revenge,* was run aground at Beaufort Inlet, then known as the *Sea of Caroline,* prior to the Battle of Ocracoke. Theories suggest that many of his crew were then marooned on the islands of the Inlet. Located by marine archaeologists in 1996, relics from the ship are displayed at the Maritime Museum in Beaufort, a short jaunt on Highway 70 across the bridge from Morehead City. The museum is a must see for any would-be mariner or history buff, and a great spot to begin or conclude your paddle from Front Street.

Beaufort, originally known as *Fish Towne,* is North Carolina's third oldest town, having been incorporated in 1722. It is home to the Rachel Carson Estuary (named for the author of the environmental classic, *Silent Spring*), a component of the North Carolina National Estuarine Research Reserve, which can be seen from the docks. Among the many houses that date back to the early 1700s is the Hammock House, circa 1709, which claims Blackbeard as one several sea captains that used the residence for occasional accommodations. The notorious buccaneer allegedly was angered by his 18 year-old French common-law wife while living at the home and hung her by the neck on an oak tree in the backyard. Legend or fact? No one can say for sure. The house is privately owned but is only a short walk from the visitor center and can be viewed from street level. During the Civil War Union officers were quartered there. Another must see is the old burying ground, which includes the grave of a young girl who died at sea and was buried in a rum keg.

Launch your vessel from anywhere along Front Street and make a 15 minute crossing of Taylor's Creek to Carrot Island. Keep going and you will soon encounter numerous uninhabited beaches and an environment that resembles what the Carolina coast must have looked like hundreds of years before. Beaufort has little competition when it comes to island hopping capabilities. Carrot Island is home to a herd of what are thought to be Spanish Mustangs that have roamed wild for centuries, and can often be seen foraging from the dock. The Carson reserve includes 2,675 acres suitable for hiking, shelling, or simply exploring the natural salt flats and eelgrass beds. Only accessible by boat, the area features more than 200 species of birds at various times throughout the year. It is hard to imagine a more convenient modern day wilderness experience via paddle.

Beach your vessel for a picnic lunch or bottle of wine and then wander through the maritime forest on a treasure hunt to seek relics from a marooned buccaneer...this is barrier island wilderness at its best. If you choose to continue, the Cape Lookout National Seashore beckons on the opposite side of the estuary. Turn your compass to the north and you might locate Gilligan on one of the many undeveloped islands that you will encounter. Take a few hours or a few days, as the seashore encompasses 56 miles of unspoiled barrier islands. You may not find a cache of doubloons, but testaments to the past abound from shark teeth to encapsulated derringers. The latter was discovered by our son Dylan on a 2004 voyage to an unnamed island, and most certainly belonged to some pirate captain back in the day. Okay, well maybe. Shackelford Banks offers an abundance of wild horses and wildlife encounters, but you will be hard pressed to find a telephone. Be aware of the weather and the tidal flow, and take the fishing rods.

Turn the compass to the south and you will see Fort Macon State Park on the eastern end of Bogue Banks. The fort, active through World War II, is well preserved and dates back to 1756. Civil War buffs probably know that the Confederate Army seized the remarkably well-preserved fort in 1861, only to see it recaptured during General John Parke's campaign (see the Hoophole Creek commentary later in this section). It can be accessed by canoe, but better take the car over the bridge so as not to be swamped by the wake of the predominant motor boats.

A trip to Beaufort would not be complete without a visit "Down East." Contrary to the uninformed popular belief, US 70 continues for miles into the easternmost part of the Cape Lookout National Seashore. The Core Sound offers many access points that beckon to the paddler in areas such as Harkers Island, Sealevel and Drum Inlet. The Cedar Island National Wildlife Refuge is perhaps the jewel of the region, and you can put in on the creek just next to the ferry. Just follow highway 70 until it ends, and then NC 12 until your road turns into waterway. From the island the Pamlico Sound resembles a calm ocean, with incredible sunsets that seem to naturally enhance when viewed from your canoe. Other than a few beach houses, particularly on the north end, one might think that time has stood still for centuries. Hopefully this area will escape the commercial homogenization that has beset so many areas of Atlantic coastal paradise.

Before you leave the vicinity, be sure to visit Atlantic Beach and canoe or kayak across Bogue Sound on the south side of the Highrise Bridge. Next to the Atlantic Station shopping center off of Fort Macon Road, you will find a historical marker that pays tribute to Giovannie de Verrazano. Long before the days of Blackbeard, Verrazano was hired by King Francis I of France to explore the coast from Canada to Florida. He found a string of islands that he named Arcadia, meaning "for the beauty of the trees." The explorer thought he was in Asia when he was actually between Cape Fear and Cape Lookout, thought to be present-day Atlantic Beach and Morehead City. He described the area as having beautiful fields and broad plains, covered with immense forests various in color, too delightful and charming to be described.

The Atlantic Beach area of Bogue Sound also played host to a crossing of the Union Army on March 29, 1862, as forces under General John G. Parke came ashore at what is now known as Hoophole Creek. The Clean Water Management Fund has funded the preservation of this area as a Coastal Nature Preserve, and a trail to the sound is suitable for a short portage of your kayak. You can find the trail just next to the Coral Bay Shopping Center, marked by a Civil War Trails display. Don't forget to look for civil war musket balls along the shore amongst the scattering hermit crabs and oyster beds.

Continue South along NC 58 towards Emerald Isle and Swansboro and more opportunities to dip the paddle can easily be found. This area, akin to Beaufort, hints of times past when life was simple. The salty tang in the air still summons paddlers to the White Oak River, just as it did when privateer Captain Otway Burns was serving colonial America during the War of 1812. The grave of Captain Burns can also be found in Beaufort, but he was a native son of what was then known as Swannsborough. Access the White Oak River at Cedar Point and paddle upstream along the salt marsh until you reach the canals along the Tideland Trail. Before you depart, don't forget Hammocks Beach State Park with ferry service from Swansboro if you wish to kayak or canoe alongside more of North Carolina's beautiful unspoiled beaches. Getting to Bear Island, a gem of the park, can only be done by boat and is roughly a 2.5 mile paddle if you forgo the ferry.

Most of you probably know the difference between men such as Captain Burns, a privateer, and Captain Teach, a pirate (for the most part). Privateers were commissioned on behalf of their local governing body, or at least supposedly, while pirates would pillage and plunder for the benefit of themselves and their crew. The Carolina coast saw many of each breed. Many names of destinations within the Outer Banks hearken back to the pirate era. For example, Kill Devil Hills was allegedly christened as such due to the rum that would wash ashore after shipwrecks, which was foul enough to "kill the devil." In addition, Nags Head was a moniker derived from a pirate's ruse of tying a lantern to a horse to lure unsuspecting ships ashore.

Blackbeard, ever the illustrious buccaneer, traversed throughout the Eastern Seaboard from Pennsylvania to the Caribbean. Although he owes much of his infinite notoriety to his blockade of Charles Town Harbor (present-day Charleston, S.C.), North Carolina holds the distinction of being home to his only "permanent" residence. That would be historic Bath, which later became our first incorporated town in 1705. Perhaps we should visit there prior to resuming our coastal exploration.

Located approximately 45 miles inland just off the Pamlico River, the legendary pirate actually attempted to become a law-abiding citizen while a resident of the town. If you paddle to Plum Point at the corner of Bath Creek and the Pamlico, you can see what are believed to be the foundational remains of the home that he and his fourteenth wife, sixteen year-old Mary Ormond, shared. Just across the bay on the west side sat the home of colonial Governor Charles Eden, who befriended the pirate. Plum Point is clearly visible from the waterfront, an area locally known as Bonner Point, and can be accessed by canoe in less than an hour.

History abounds at Bonner Point as well, which is where East Carolina University students have conducted extensive archaeological excavations. This is the locale where the legendary John Lawson chose to build his home, circa 1706. John's claim to fame may be as surveyor-general, but he also holds title as being the first author of the history of Carolina in 1709. But before Lawson, there were pirates in the vicinity.

Governor Eden had granted the King's pardon to Blackbeard less than a month after Capt. Teach had conducted his highly profitable blockade of Charleston. Some say that Blackbeard had brought upwards of 1500 pounds sterling with him to Bath Town, and many have been digging and metal detecting the snake and mosquito infested areas surrounding the creek for years. Governor Eden actually conducted the Anglican marriage ceremony between Teach and Ormond, and was often accused of being in "cahoots" with the pirate and a beneficiary of his plundering ways.

Historic Bath can be found just east of Little Washington, off of NC 92. A visitor's center is staffed full of friendly locals who will be happy to assist you. Don't miss St. Thomas Episcopal Church on Craven Street, the oldest European place of worship in the state, dating back to 1734. Also drop by the Palmer-Marsh House on Main Street which dates back to 1751 and entertained the likes of the Marquis de Lafayette, among other notables. Bath Creek runs right alongside Main and is only a short paddle from confluence with the Pamlico. When he left Bath to return to pirating, legend has it that Blackbeard cursed the town, forbidding it from growing any larger than it was during his time there. 17th century Bath boasted a population of some 8,000 people, but today less than 300 residents call it home.

If you make your way to Bath, don't neglect to paddle Goose Creek. The State Park lies only a few miles west on highway 92 (en route to Washington), with an entrance just off state road 1334. There is a developed camping area that sits creekside with numerous points from which to launch your canoe or kayak. Head south and you will soon reach the Pamlico just after Flatty Creek appears on your left, another must see segment of your paddling expedition. Be wary of the many Osprey nests that predominate among the Bald Cypress or you could be dive bombed by an angry raptor. A pleasant afternoon can be spent simply floating along and watching those intriguing fish hawks catch their evening meal with their talons. Fishing in the brackish water is excellent as well and a variety of species, from Redfish to Largemouth Bass, can readily be caught.

On a final note, particularly if you are fortunate enough to bring along a preschool paddler, continue on to Washington and visit the North Carolina Estaurarium on the banks of the Pamlico. The intricate world of the marine biologist awaits the young explorer, and you can always drop your canoe from the dock and paddle downstream into the estuary. Although slightly influenced by the tide, this segment of the Pamlico offers flatwater with little current for an easy roundtrip.

More coastal area paddling sites abound in this wonderfully undeveloped section of the state, but first let's revisit the seaboard.

B. A Lost Colony and the Outer Banks

Enough about the pirates, North Carolina has other colonial era legends to explore. Roanoke Island was not only home to John White's village of mystery, but also to the Freedman's Colony, a haven for runaway slaves during the Civil War. The island served as host to a battle between the Union and Confederacy, and remnants of forts from that era can still be seen on the western side of the island. Put in at the public ramp at the end of Bowser Town Road and paddle north for a day trip that will take you not only on a voyage through history but also to the state aquarium, a destination that can cause adults to be kids again (*Editors note: North Carolina is home to two additional coastal aquariums, located at Pine Knoll Shores and Fort Fisher).

The story of the Lost Colony is one that pervades western civilization classes from elementary school through advanced graduate study. Although Roanoke has endured over four centuries of change since the disappearance of the settlers, it is still possible to envision the environment within which these brave individuals attempted to gain a foothold. Paddle along the waterfront of Manteo in Shallowbag Bay and you will see the Elizabeth II, a replica of one of the three ships that brought 110 colonists to the island in July of 1587. Paddle on the north end of the island and living history continues in a less cosmopolitan setting...the remains of Fort Raleigh.

The "New Forte in Vergina" is the only structure connected to the Lost Colony whose site has been exactly located through the efforts of extensive excavations beginning in 1936. The national historic site can be viewed by kayak or canoe from the Roanoke Sound, and trails through a quiet wooded area lead to the site and Elizabethan Gardens. Colonizing the New World was a fervent dream of Sir Walter Raleigh, and he received a charter from Queen Elizabeth in 1584 to explore doing just that. The initial expedition to Roanoke Island sent by our capitol city's namesake arrived the following year and built the fort. Conditions rapidly deteriorated due to food shortages and problems with the local natives, but fortunately the privateer Sir Francis Drake happened along to rescue the party and return them to England.

In 1587 Sir Walter sent out yet another group to Roanoke which included men, women and children. The colony's governor, John White, was an artist by profession and left in pictures and text the first depictions of our country's east coast wilderness areas. All surviving original drawings are showcased at the print room of the British Museum in London, but can be accessed online thanks to an agreement with the staff of *Virtual Jamestown*. My personal favorite à his watercolor entitled "Indians Fishing" that shows native Secotan Indians, thought to be of the Algonquin Nation, paddling their cypress dugout canoe along the sound.

Returning to the story, Governor White soon departed for England to obtain additional supplies.

Unfortunately, war had broken out with Spain and his return to Roanoke was delayed for three years. When he finally arrived back in Roanoke there were no settlers to be found. He saw no sign of violence, fortifications and homes were intact, but 116 people were missing. His only clue was the word CROATOAN carved into a tree and CRO carved into another that stood nearby. Theories abound as to what happened to the settlement, which included young Virginia Dare, known to all as White's granddaughter and the first child born of English parents in the New World. Perhaps some modern day paddler will happen along some additional item of archaeological evidence and help supply a piece of the ancient puzzle?

It's time to remember that this *is* a book about paddling, albeit in a historical context, but justice will not attempt to be effectively rendered to the many sites of visitor interest within the Cape Hatteras National Seashore (Wright Brothers Memorial, Jockey's Ridge, Bodie and Hatteras Lighthouses, just to name a few). The local chambers of commerce can help you out along those lines if you are in tourist mode. As for paddling, after the experience of Roanoke, you may ready for some higher degree of solitude when you next hit the water. Cross over the bridge and head toward Kitty Hawk along US 158. You may wish to stop off for a hike or paddle along the sound adjacent to Nags Head Woods at Kill Devil Hills, or you may prefer to continue to milepost 1/4 just before reaching the Wright Memorial Bridge. The narrow waterway that appears is known as Jean Guite Creek, home to otters, herons, egrets, and a variety of reptiles. Giant crepe myrtle trees provide a canopy along the route which adjoins the Kitty Hawk Forest Preserve. Paddle north towards Southern Shores and you will soon leave civilization behind.

If you would rather take a southern route and begin the trek towards Ocracoke, the Pea Island Wildlife Refuge is a must for paddling in a natural habitat. The refuge is located on Hatteras Island and extends from Oregon Inlet south to the village of Rodanthe. Just follow NC 12 and you will pass several parking areas with trail and/or boat access. Ocean beaches, barrier dunes, salt marshes, fresh and brackish water ponds, tidal creeks, and bays can all be found within the boundaries of this contemporary Eden, but the crown jewel may be the 25,700 acres of Pamlico Sound waters. Snow geese, tundra swans, bald eagles and peregrine falcons are but a few of the migratory waterfowl and raptors who call this area on the Atlantic Flyway a temporary home.

Just south of Eagle Nest Bay paddlers will thrill to the natural beauty and mesmerizing sunsets on the waters of North Pond, North Field Pond, and South Pond. You would think that the powers that be could have come up with more unique names for these picturesque remnants of coastal wilderness. Why not Sir Francis Pond? Peregrine Field? Oh well, maybe those aren't much better after all. New Inlet, just past the visitor station on highway 12, also affords a great spot to launch your canoe or kayak into Pamlico Sound.

The Pea Island area is thought to be the locale where Sir Walter Raleigh (yep, same guy), sent a small exploring expedition a few years prior to his colonizing efforts. The story goes that on the third day of their stay on what was then known as Hatarask Island, three Indians in a canoe appeared. They seemed afraid of the giant ship and the strange beings inside it, but the Englishmen persuaded one of them to come aboard. He was promptly given a shirt, hat, and a couple drinks of wine. Wine in lieu of rum? Something must be wrong here, but it worked out just the same. The native soon returned with a load of fish from his dugout for the Europeans. This led to a visit from the chief's brother, Granganimeo, and a friendship that was probably more genuine than that enjoyed by the Pilgrims. It further served as an impetus for the Fort Raleigh expedition.

How nice it is to still be able to see this area in a form similar to what it must have resembled over 400 years ago! No condominiums, no roller coasters, just solitude and shipwrecks in the surf and beyond. Several parking areas off of highway 12 will house your vehicle as you put in to paddle the *Graveyard of the Atlantic*. From 1650 through 1850 over 2,000 ships found their way to the bottom of the ocean thanks to North Carolina's dreaded shoals and shifting sand bars, hence the name. Keep in mind that this is a barrier island, and in the warmer months it shares the trademark weather patterns of the tropics, i.e. thunderstorms and riptide currents. Although shoals and sand bars don't generally serve as hazards for the paddler, the surf can be dangerous. Accordingly, be aware of current conditions and take necessary precautions.

The Cape Hatteras National Seashore is a national treasure and one of the many natural areas that make our state so unique for many outdoor activities. Books can be and have been written about this area alone, so I will leave you to consult with them and take our boats further south for a final segment on coastal paddling.

C. The Cape Fear Region

Don't let Robert De Niro scare you away from a visit to the southeastern corner of our coast. *Cape Fear* is more than just a movie. Dominated by the historic port city of Wilmington, days could be spent touring what has become the Carolina's most populous coastal region. You are, however, only about an hour or so from the Grand Strand and Myrtle Beach, so watch out for the company of power boats and spring breakers on jet skis. No offense, but some of those characters seem to enjoy annoying even the most tolerant of paddlers. The majority, however, will properly cut the engine and minimize wake. Be sure to hit their waves at an angle so as to limit the chance of a standing wave sending you into an unexpected swim.

The remains of Fort Fisher, site of the largest land/sea battle of the Civil War in 1865, can be viewed by sea kayak or canoe at Kure Beach. Before its fall to the Union, the fort protected blockade runners en route to Wilmington with supplies vital to the Confederate armies. It was the largest of the earthen fortifications in the Confederacy during the war, the remains of which are well preserved.

Paddle along the wharf in Wilmington and you will find many restored 18th century homes, together with the World War II battleship *North Carolina*, who participated in every major offensive naval battle in the Pacific Theater and earned 15 battle stars. While gawking at the 728 foot ship, be sure to stay close to shore and avoid the waves from the omnipresent commercial vessels. You may not find the same degree of wilderness that points further north may offer, but the occasional shallow inlet that only the paddler can access will lead to a nice respite for a picnic. Be sure to conclude whatever trip you embark upon with a meal in Brunswick County's Calabash, a small town whose reputation has led to the creation of "Calabash style" seafood restaurants throughout the southeastern United States. Arrive early enough in the day to put in on the Calabash River, head north along the edge of the marsh, and bring your fishing gear.

The intracoastal waterway has many tidal creeks to be discovered in the Wrightsville and Carolina beach areas, and many public access points can be found throughout the region. One of the better venues for the "wilderness paddler" would be Carolina Beach State Park, just off US 421 to the right as you approach the beach town city limit. Home to the renowned cannibal of the horticultural world, the Venus Flytrap, the park offers the opportunity to hike through a maritime forest and see the Flytrap in its natural element. Given that the species grows wild only in bogs and savannah environments within a 100 mile radius of Wilmington, you can take advantage of what most only view when visiting their local Lowe's or nursery chain. While there, be sure to paddle Snows Cut, which meanders through the park from the intracoastal to Myrtle Grove Sound. Further north you will reach the undeveloped wilderness of Masonboro Coastal Reserve which borders the waterway and offers yet another undeveloped chain of barrier islands to explore. Again, be sure check your tide tables and perhaps seek some guidance from the local ranger regarding time frame and destination points.

Not far from Wilmington lies the 2,757 acre hammock of Roan Island, which adjoins abandoned rice fields in an area flanked by both the Cape Fear and Black Rivers. Thanks to the Nature Conservancy, a large majority of the island will live forever in a blissful state of coastal wilderness. Only a boat will get you there, as no bridge connects directly to the island. From US 421, turn left on NC 210 and head west past Moore's Creek Battlefield (see description in the next section). After crossing the Black River, take a left on Canetuck Road (SR 1104) and then a quick left on Heading Bluff Road (SR 1103). Small boat access can be found at the Lyon's Creek bridge in about 2 miles. Paddle downstream (southeast) on Lyon's and the island will soon appear. Turn right and the creek will merge into the Cape Fear, or take a left and you will soon be paddling the Black. A former logging area, the isolated Roan is now home to black bear, deer, bobcat, alligator, and incredible fishing. The rivers do remain tidal in this area as well.

Just north of the Wilmington area lies Topsail Island, a relic of coastal preservation unto itself. Topsail is family friendly, 26 miles from north to south, and offers generally calm waterways from which you can explore the inlet. Much of Topsail remains as it were from the days of my childhood, and it is easy to find many paddle "put in" sites along the sound side road. It is a short venture across the open water to enter a realm of wilderness, home to the blue crabs and clams that predominate the habitat. The salt marsh serves as a natural barrier between the sound and the intracoastal, creating an atmosphere that should remain free of commercial interference.

Further north along NC 50 you will find Surf City, known more for its saltwater fishing reputation as opposed to the Beach Boy or Jan and Dean surfers. Keep going straight on NC 210, pass through North Topsail, and you will soon cross the intracoastal. Drop your paddle at the public access area on the inland side of the bridge. From there you can paddle north among the marsh to Alligator Bay or south towards Goose Bay, generally without a significant power boat presence. Salt marsh wilderness is abundant in both directions of this area that is among the least developed within the Cape Fear region. Time to continue further inland.

Merchants Millpond

Chapter Two:

Let's Go Swampin'

*"Nature bears the close inspection
of an insect's eye view"*

—Henry David Thoreau

North Carolina may not have the Okefenokee, but a seemingly endless string of cypress-dominant swamp forests dot the Coastal Plain from north to south. These areas contain some of the oldest bald cypress in the world, a benefit from being somewhat removed in terms of accessibility from efficient logging operations. These giant trees served to furnish the earliest canoes known to exist in the Carolinas, some of which can be seen at Lake Phelps, one of several natural "bay lakes" of the central coastal plain. Bring the bug spray and we'll begin with that mysterious region of our coastal inland paddling haven.

A. Asteroid, Star Wars or Peat Bog Fire?

Some canoe buffs such as yours truly enjoy a historical quest to not only paddle into history, but also to nourish an inherent appreciation for the origins of the opportunity to do so. To that end, you may wish to visit the impressive display of wood/canvas and birchbark canoes that can be found at the Adirondack Museum in Blue Mountain, New York, or for that matter the Canadian Canoe Museum in Peterborough, Ontario. The Golden Lake Algonquin First Nation Community in Ontario likewise exhibits traditional birchbark paddle craft, some of which date back to the 1850s.

For those who would rather not venture so far from home, a significant portion of such history can be found in our own backyard. The Objibway, Huron, Micmac, and other northeastern tribes may lay claim to the remarkable invention of the birchbark canoe, just as the French fur traders bear responsibility for its adaption from a bark base to wood/canvas. However, long before either invention, in coastal Carolina, the Tuscarora,

Croatan, and others burned and scraped giant cypress into dugout canoes. Heavy but functional, the dugouts were used for hunting, fishing, and basic transportation through our swamps and rivers.

At Pettigrew State Park, seven miles south of Creswell off of US 64, we find North Carolina's second largest natural lake and an impressive number of ancient dugouts. Lake Phelps lies off a vast peninsula between the Albemarle Sound and Pamlico River, and is thought to be over 38,000 years old. Scientists have long debated the mystery of how the bay lakes formed, and have proposed many theories. Causation has been attributed to underground springs, wind and wave action from a prehistoric coastline, meteor showers, glacial activity, and peat burn, but none of these hypotheses has gained universal acceptance. One thing is for certain, this massive lake offers a glimpse into the relationship between human culture and nature going back over 10,000 years.

Although archaeologists have uncovered thousands of pottery fragments and projectile points, the most fascinating discovery is a collection of over 30 dugout canoes which are believed to have been sunk by seasonal native American hunters in the lake's shallow water. One of the canoes is 37 feet in length, the longest known dugout to exist in the southeast. Another has been carbon dated to be 4,380 years old. With the exception of a few at the visitor center and one at the Museum of History in Raleigh, the canoes remain in the lake which serves to protect against their dissipation. Some are temporarily removed for display at the park's annual Indian Heritage Celebration.

Lake Phelps boasts over 16,600 acres of water to explore. Several manmade canals enter on the north/northeast shore, and it is generally easy to find a spot to launch for paddling. A boat ramp can be found near Somerset Place, a state historic site and plantation from the ante-bellum south. Civil War buffs can visit the grave of Confederate General James Johnston Pettigrew just off the old carriage road. Gen. Pettigrew, the park's namesake, led the North Carolina 26th regiment in the high-water mark charge at Gettysburg. He died there-after after being wounded during General Robert E. Lee's retreat following the battle.

Nestled amidst this "blackwater country," and rising from the wetlands of Lake Phelps, you will find the legendary Scuppernong River. Meandering through some 26 miles of swamp forest, the river is thought to have begun some 4,000 years ago, increasing in size as the climate warmed. European farmers arrived in the 1600s, and African-American slaves eventually dug a canal connecting the lake to the river which offered agrarian products an outlet for export to the merchant sailors who waited downstream.

The Scuppernong is generally comfortable (temperature & mosquito-wise that is) year-round, and offers little to no current with an abundance of relatively undeveloped and remote inland wilderness. A favorite short trek is to put-in at Riders Creek off SR 1105 and paddle a little over 2 miles to the Columbia waterfront, which makes for an easy bicycle return shuttle. For a longer adventure, you can begin at either Spruill's Bridge off SR 1142 (15.5 miles to Columbia), or Cross Landing (9.5 miles to Columbia), all of which offer greenway paddling through a swamp forest of cypress, juniper and gum. A short distance from the river the forest gives way to *pocosins,* unique shrub bogs built upon layers of peat. The name ironically is one of several attributed to the

Alonquians, and translates into *"swamp on a hill."*

The Mattamuskeet National Wildlife Refuge can be found a short crow's fly to the southeast of Pettigrew, and boasts the 40,000 acre centerpiece known as Lake Mattamuskeet. Native Americans hold claim to designating the lake to be known as *"Mata-mackya-t-wi"*, which means "moving swamp." Lake Mattamuskeet is a true paddlers dream, 18 miles long, 5 to 6 miles wide, and only averages approximately 2 feet in depth. A former hunting ground of the Algonquians, the lake provides a valuable wintering refuge for thousands of snowbirds, including geese and tundra swans that travel along the Atlantic Flyway.

Drive east from Belhaven along US 264, or south from Columbia on highway 94, and the lake will seemingly appear out of nowhere. NC 94 divides the lake in half and offers boat access just before your reach the southern shoreline. Other access points abound along the lakeshore, just don't forget to bring the rod and reel for world-class largemouth bass angling. Deer, bobcat, otters, and the occasional black bear are among the 'critters that call the refuge home. Words cannot begin to describe the beauty of this remote paddling paradise, which represents the ultimate in family-friendly wilderness of the coastal plain.

Further inland yet another refuge beckons to the paddler. The Alligator River National Wildlife Refuge encompasses over 150,000 acres of wetland habitat that is home to a tremendous variety of wildlife species, ranging from the alligator to the relocated and thriving red wolf, brought back from the brink of extinction. Keep north on highway 94 from Mattamuskeet and you will pass through the Pocosin Lakes National Wildlife Refuge while en route to Columbia. Take a right on US 64, head east and cross the Albemarle Sound. A right on Buffalo City Road will take you to the refuge headquarters (*note that this trip could also be a great stop off point during your return from the Roanoke/Outer Banks area discussed in the previous chapter).

Milltail Creek traverses the heart of the seemingly road-less refugee, and you can paddle a variety of water trails ranging from about 1.5 to 5.5 miles. Sawyer Lake also represents a nice day trip, but you may run into a motorboat or two, not to mention a hunting party if in season. Be sure to bring the insect repellant unless you're on a mid-winter foray.

Last but not least, discussion of Carolina "swamp-ventures" would be incomplete absent mention of the 159,000+ acre Croatan National Forest. When you zoom by along US 70 en route to the beach, it is easy to miss the small visitor center set back among the tall pines that line the highway. Consider it as a hidden gateway to a world away. Longleaf pine savannas once dominated the coastal plain of the southeastern United States, but 98 percent of them are gone due to logging and the emerging dominance of other species. The Croatan harbors some remaining strands from the colonial era (up to 300 years old), and in 2002 the Forest Service embarked upon a plan that calls for restoration of the landscape to pre-European settlement conditions! A great idea, but no need to wait for the complete transformation, as the national forest offers unique paddling opportunities every day of the year right now.

Lake paddlers can choose from Catfish Lake (access off of FR 158), Great Lake (off FR 126), or the adjoining Long, Little and Ellis Lakes. All are approximately 10 miles west of Havelock as the crow flies. Public boat ramps also provide access to the Neuse and White Oak Rivers, in addition to Cahooque and Brice Creeks. The latter is a favorite pilgrimage, beginning in the Sheep Ridge Wilderness and following north to its juncture with the Trent River just south of New Bern. A popular put-in is the Wildlife Resource Commission access on FR 121-A, which offers a downstream paddle of approximately 2.5 miles to the Trent. For more seclusion, try the Lee's Bridge crossing off of FR 111.

Other area swamp ventures are out there and too numerous to count, including the Tar River and Contentnea Creek areas near Greenville. Pirate fans (of the East Carolina University gender that is), may wish to obtain the Pitt County paddle trail map which includes several different access points and nearby destinations. If interested, contact the Pamlico-Tar River Foundation (info@ptrf.org) for more detailed information.

B.   The Enchanted Forest, a Northeastern Land of Lore and Legend

The father of our country, that same guy who chopped down the old Cherry Tree, was truly an ecologist at heart. George himself described the Great Dismal Swamp in May of 1763 as "a glorious paradise…neither plain nor hollow, but a hillside." Washington orchestrated the surveying and digging of the 5-mile ditch from the western edge of the swamp to Lake Drummond, a lovely circular body of water that covers approximately 3,000 acres. The swamp itself originally spread over nearly 2200 square miles, but due to clearing and drainage for cultivation purposes, the current size stands at approximately 600 miles. It's simple to drop paddle in the canal at the Dismal Swamp Canal Visitor Center on US 17 in South Mills, which allows for a blackwater outing in either direction. Why is the water black? Actually it's amber-colored and unusually pure, preserved by tannic acids that prohibit bacteria from growing in the water. Before the days of refrigeration, water from the swamp was a highly prized commodity on sailing ships since it would remain fresh within the kegs for a long time.

A land of mystical folklore, the tale perhaps best known is the Lady of the Lake, canonized by Irish poet Thomas Moore in 1803. Locals say that an Indian maiden who died just before her wedding day is periodically seen paddling her ghostly white canoe across the waters of the swamp. Moore's poem, "The Lake of the Dismal Swamp," tells how her bereaved lover came to believe that his lost love had departed her grave and taken to the swamp. He followed her and never returned, reuniting with her as they continue to paddle as one spirit. Other ghosts abound, primarily due to the Civil War Battle of South Mills in 1862 which eventually enabled the Union to capture control of this important transportation route. Thereafter, a number of Confederate deserters hid out in the swamp and made occasional raids on federal boats. In December of 1863, General Edward A. Wild attempted to capture the rebels and in the process burned settlements, hung innocent men, and took women as hostages. Such action led North Carolina Governor Zebulon B. Vance, a native of Weaverville, to refer to Wild as a "disgrace to the manhood of the age."

The swamp is brimming with colonial history, and mention must be made of its service as a natural refuge for runaway slaves. Following the American Revolution, many fleeing African-Americans chose to join a colony of "maroons" in the swamp, which was at the time such an inhospitable place that sanctuary came naturally. The actions of a few, however, who preyed on unwary swamp travelers, caused much alarm among residents living near the swamp. In 1831, a brutal slave uprising lead by Nat Turner resulted in the butchering of 55 men, women and children in a community known as Courtland, Virginia. Similar unrest had been reported in nearby Camden and Elizabeth City, North Carolina. A militia force, complete with dogs, was thereby sent to wipe out the runaway slave colonies, and many were killed. In 1842, Henry Wadsworth Longfellow memorialized this chapter in the swamp's dismal past with his poem, "The Slave in Dismal Swamp."

While in the area, journey east of Elizabeth City to an often overlooked blackwater stream known as Indiantown Creek. The Camden County Chamber of Commerce publishes a trail map that includes Indiantown, which covers some 30,000 acres of North River Game Land and is adjacent to our Wildlife Resource Commission's black bear sanctuary. Some of North Carolina's last remaining virgin bald cypress and Atlantic White Cedar can be visited in this primeval coastal wilderness, which represents an immediate escape from contemporary urban society. The trail begins as a drainage canal on SR 1148, but a public landing off Indiantown Road is more accessible. It is possible to continue downstream to the North River and take out at Coinjock along the Intracoastal Waterway, but that makes for a long day given a distance of approximately 15 miles or so. Accordingly, you may wish to plan for an out and back day trip. The trail is well marked thanks to its identification as part of the Albemarle Region Canoe and Small Boat Trails System.

Perhaps my favorite paddle within the region features a forest befitting the wizards and druids from whence its name is evoked: The "Enchanted Forest" of Merchants Millpond State Park. Directions to the forest are whimsical—take the canoe trail to the campsites, then follow the yellow buoys through the millpond, turn right at the last island, bear left at the beaver lodge, paddle along the shoreline, find a channel into Lassiter Swamp, then head straight until morning. Even in the light of day the forest stirs primordial instinct and casts a spell, but in reality the paddle is only about 2 miles from the millpond put in. Trees have never been cut in this ancient grove, where thousand-year-old bald cypress mingle with tupelo gums, while Spanish moss drapes their canopy.

Often described as being a cross between Florida's Everglades and Georgia's Okefenokee, the centerpiece of the park is the pond itself, which was formed in 1811 when Bennett's Creek was dammed to power a gristmill. At only 3,250 acres, the relatively small park is home to one of the most diverse collections of plant and animal life in the mid-Atlantic, from beaver to bear to the poisonous cottonmouth. Over 200 varieties of birds and mammals, together with approximately 70 species of amphibians and reptiles and 150 assorted water plants, watch as visiting paddlers invade their ecological wonderland.

Merchants Millpond is easy to reach from US 158 and lies between the communities of Gatesville and Sunbury. It is approximately 30 miles from the towns of Ahoskie, Elizabeth City, and Edenton. A family canoe-in campground is available for an overnight stay, and don't be surprised if inquisitive otters play hide and seek with your crew as you paddle in. Primitive camping is also available, and canoes may be rented if necessary. Family-friendly hiking trails surround the pond if you wish to beach the boat and enjoy a diversionary land excursion. Do yourself a favor and don't miss this "can't miss" of experiences within the coastal plain arena.

As with each section of this book, other paddling destinations abound within the area. Civil War buffs should paddle the Roanoke River in the Hamilton area and visit Fort Branch. Overlooking the river off of SR 1416, this Confederate Earthen Fort features eight original cannons among other displays from the era. The upper Perquimans River put-in at Missing Mill Park makes for a convenient wilderness day trip if you paddle north, and upon return be sure to drop by Hertford and admire the many 1700-era structures that lie at the head of the tidewater section of the river.

Outfitters operate day trips from the Historic Edenton waterfront along Queen Anne's Creek and Pembroke Creek, either of which can be run as an out and back day trip. An upstream paddle on the Chowan River, or a trip along the shoreline of the Albemarle Sound, present additonal options for the paddler to consider. Tourists will enjoy Edenton, a quaint coastal town that became the adopted home of Joseph Hewes,who, although not a native Carolinian, was an original signatory to the Declaration of Independence.

Just north of Rocky Mount off of US 301, on the south bank of the Roanoke River, you will find more colonial history in the former port town of Halifax. North Carolina's Fourth Provincial Congress met here in the spring of 1776, and on April 12 delegates unanimously enacted the first legislation by an original colony that called for independence from England. Who knew at the time that within two months the entire nation would follow suit? Ironically, the first reading of the U.S. Declaration occurred at the Halifax Courthouse site on August 1, 1776. Public river access is no longer available in Halifax, but at the visitor center one of the volunteers, clad in 1700-era attire, can direct you to points upstream at Weldon or downstream near Scotland Neck. The Roanoke is known for some potential hazards so be sure to seek local advice before dropping the paddle.

C.   Redcoats and Alligators in the Southeast

Journey back to February 27, 1776, and paddle into the history of the Battle of Moore's Creek Bridge. Follow Highway 421 about 20 miles northwest from Wilmington, then go west on NC 210 for 5 miles into the National Park. Put in off the park road near the picnic area and listen closely for the ghostly sounds of the fife and drum core as they echo through the forest, which remains relatively undeveloped in this remote area of farmland. It is a short paddle to the reconstructed bridge, where a group of approximately 150 Patriots under Colonels Alexander Lillington and Richard Caswell defeated a larger force of Loyalists in a battle that effectively ended royal authority in the colony. The creek, a tributary of the Black River, winds through swampy terrain which at the time could only be crossed by use of the bridge. Lillington's troops arrived at the bridge a day ahead of the Loyalists and prepared earthworks on the high ground across from the bridge, the remnants of which can be still be seen today. When the Loyalists attacked their broadswords were met with a barrage of musket and artillery fire, leaving some 30 dead. The Patriots suffered only one casualty, and locals say that his apparition can still be seen haunting the swamp during a full moon.

After the Patriot victory at Moore's Creek, the Fourth North Carolina Provincial Congress met in Halifax. On April 12, 1776, members unanimously adopted the Halifax Resolves, which ordered the North Carolina Delegation in Philadelphia to seek and vote for independence. This action made our state the first of the colonial governments to call for independence, and the signing date of the instrument remains today as one of two that appears on the North Carolina flag *(the other being April 12, 1776, when the Mecklenburg Resolves, aka Mecklenburg Declaration of Independence, was promulgated).*

Just up the road from Moore's Creek paddlers will find the Northeast Cape Fear River in Pender County. Take exit 398 off of Interstate 40, then NC 53 East to County Road 1512, which dead ends at the access point. Take a right around the bend at the put in and venture upstream to Holly Shelter Creek, which enters on the left after about a half mile. If you continue up the main channel of the Northeast Cape, the mouth of Ashes Creek will soon appear on your left. Both Holly Shelter and Ashes allow for an optional course of exploration, and each offers side channels in both directions that only a canoe or kayak can navigate. This area offers terrific solitude and only a negligible amount of motorboat traffic (encounters occur more often downstream of the put in), but be wary of area hunters if you're out on a day other than the Sabbath.

The water is a mystical dark tea color, owing to the tannic acid that permeates most rivers and creeks in North Carolina's coastal plain. Thanks to the juniper, gum, and cypress trees, bacteria cannot grow in the water. Before the days of refrigeration, the water was thought to be chemically pure and if regularly drunk would promote long life. I don't know about magical qualities, but together with the abundance of Spanish moss the area sure does seem reminiscent of the Georgia/Florida wonderland known as Okefenokee.

While in the area be sure to visit Lake Waccamaw, a timeless treasure that is another one of North Carolina's unique bay lakes. Tourists seem to whiz by this Columbus County natural wonder in a hurry to get to the Cape Fear beaches, but the lake is only a short detour off of US 74. Turn right on NC 214 just past Whiteville and you will be on Lake Shore Drive within minutes. The road does not encompass the entire lake, but changes names as you drive around to choose your put in location. A five mile trail runs along the south side of the lake, which encompasses approximately 9,000 acres of remarkably shallow water with an average depth of only seven feet.

Home to 52 different species of fish, some of which are found nowhere else in the world, the lake has the distinction of being home to the largest variety of finned creatures within the Old North State. Fish aren't the only native inhabitants, however, that are predominant at Lake Waccamaw. Be wary of the omnipresent alligator and water moccasin. A sizeable population of each call the area home, but most are relatively harmless if left alone. A direct descendant of the dinosaur, our Carolina gators first appeared over 250 million years ago. Keep in mind that they can outrun a human for about the equivalent of a 40 yard dash, so be sure to observe them from a safe distance. Leave your dogs at home since they represent a preferred size of prey and could make for a gourmet gator feast. If fishing, don't string your catch off the side of any canoe or kayak as a gator may claim it for an appetizer.

To explore the lake, try putting in at the state park which is located at the end of the road on the northeast shoreline amongst the limestone bluffs that rise from the swampy terrain. Canoe camping works well at the park, which requires a short portage of gear from the parking area to the camp sites. Paddlers can also access the lake at the Columbus County Access Area near the visitor center, or the Wildlife Resources Commission ramp on the west side. Be prepared to share the immediate vicinity of these latter choices with a motorboat or two. As an alternative, try the drive to the end of Waccamaw Shores Road and you will reach the spillway, which is the otherwise known as the headwaters of the Waccamaw River. This is a great spot to launch from if you tire of exploring the grass beds, cypress, and lily pads that lie along the edge of the lakeshore. The swampy river snakes its way (or should I say "moccasins" its way due to the prevalence of that deadly reptile) all the way to the Atlantic, where it enters not far from the Grand Strand. It is a perfect setting for an "out and back" day trip due to the slow current and lack of tidal influence at this point inland, but bring the mosquito repellant.

Further inland is a favorite haunt of mine that is not found on many maps or guide books, but I'll risk the local wrath by disclosing what is known as Rhoades Pond (after all, I live in the mountains now anyway). About 15 miles north of Fayetteville, just off of US 301, sits Mingo Swamp. The crown jewel of the swamp can be accessed roadside, but pay attention or you'll zoom by and miss the put-in. Locals with their cane poles line the roadside shoreline and fish for bream (aka bluegill), catfish and "jack" (aka chain pickerel), but you will soon leave them behind as you venture into the blackwater. No other roads or developed areas can be found along the shore, and towering bald cypress draped in Spanish moss rise from the waters of the pond. Rhoades Pond probably qualifies as a small lake as its size is comparable to others of such designation within the region, i.e. Holts Lake and Quaker Neck Lake, yet provides an easily accessible wilderness experience. Embark at sunrise and paddle into another dimension with twilight zone aura as the fog rises off the water. Drift along on a sultry day and ride its sluggish waters filled with duckweed— just remember that natural systems never make haste. There is a certain calm that attaches to the serenity of the setting.

A close neighbor to Rhodes is Jones Lake, yet another bay lake that lies about 15 miles south of Fayetteville within the Cape Fear basin. Take NC 53 south, then left on NC 242 and the state park will appear in about a mile. The lake is part of the state forest game land of 32,237 acres known as Bladen Lakes, and the adjacent area is swamp in all directions with primitive camping allowed. A three mile trail circuits the shoreline. Lake Singletary is a cousin lake to Jones, and also offers a state park with access off of highway 53 approximately 5 miles south of the 242 turnoff. Singletary is the deepest of North Carolina's bay lakes with a maximum depth of about 12 feet. Although relatively close to the city, both lakes represent quick and easy wilderness paddles that are perfect for a family afternoon. Due to popularity with hunters, be sure to wear orange just in case Dick Cheney is around! As of the time of this writing, North Carolina does not allow hunting on Sundays, so that day might be your safest bet.

Before we leave the coastal plain we must return to John Lawson, the maverick explorer who seems to pop up just about everywhere within the history of colonial Carolina. Unfortunately, the pioneer patriarch met an untimely death at the hands of Tuscarora Indians during a canoe voyage back in 1711 along the Neuse River. Lawson, together with associate Christopher von Graffenreid, were captured and taken as hostages to the town of Catechna (near modern day Snow Hill). After insulting, rather than placating, their captors, both were savagely murdered. The tribe eventually fled to upstate New York and ultimately became part of the Iroquois Confederacy, so one can only envision a ghostly encounter while paddling along the contemporary Neuse. What is now known as Cliffs of the Neuse State Park was once a ceremonial ground and gathering place for the Tuscarora and Saponi, and early European settlers set up a trading center at what is now known as Seven Springs.

The cliffs of the park are a rainbow of white, tan, yellow and brown, and rise approximately 90 feet above the water. Formed millions of years ago when a fault in the earth's crust shifted, they remain virtually unaltered and stand as a journal of the biological history of the area. Once you pass through Wayne County and the park area, the upstream section makes for a great inland wilderness paddle. The put-in at the NC 111 bridge to take out at Seven Springs is approximately 8 miles, but requires shuttle. As an alternative, you can launch from the park and paddle upstream at your leisure for a roundtrip. Cliffs of the Neuse State Park is located about 14 miles southeast of Goldsboro off of NC 111, and is about an hour from Raleigh.

While trekking along the Neuse, drop by the CSS Neuse State Historic Site along the waterfront in Kinston. Built in an effort to recapture Union-held New Bern, the ironclad gunboat was set afire in March of 1865. It was then sunk to avoid capture after its rebel crew shelled the advancing Union Cavalry. Another paddling opportunity would be the least developed section of Johnston County from the SR 1201 bridge to the SR 1224 crossing in Wayne County, which is only a couple of miles but takes you in the vicinity of the infamous Bentonville Battlefield. This March 19-21, 1865, altercation represents the largest Civil War battle fought on North Carolina soil. It is also known to history buffs as being the last full-scale Confederate offensive from General Joseph Johnston as he attempted to block Union Gen. William Tecumseh Sherman's march to Goldsboro.

Finally, I would be remiss if we failed to return to the river that perhaps best represents the heart of south-eastern paddling: the Cape Fear. The Cape Fear transcends much of the eastern Piedmont to the coast, and if you put in at Greensboro you can conceivably paddle all the way to the Atlantic. I don't recommend it unless you enjoy jumping over dams along the way, but there are several treks worthy of a family outing that deserve mention. Section One of the *Cape Fear Canoe Trail* is primarily flatwater, and enables you to pass by the area of a bridge erected by the redcoats of General Corwallis during the American Revolution. Put-in lies at the US 1 bridge over the Deep River, and take-out would be the NC 42 access area, a distance of approximately 8 miles.

Section two of the river is a stretch of some 16 miles, beginning at the NC 42 access and ending at the SR 2016 take-out approximately 2 miles south of Lillington. This paddle is best accompanied by an overnight camp at Raven Rock State Park, which features hiking trails and a canoe-camp area. The upper reaches of section 2 include a portage around the abandoned Buckhorn Dam on the left, and a couple of class 2 rockgardens prior to reaching the park. The "rock" of the "Raven" was originally known as Patterson's Rock, so named after an early settler who found refuge there when his canoe capsized nearby. It was changed in 1854 due to the inspiration of the numerous ravens that choose to roost along the ledges. If you paddle by, you can't help but marvel at the immense crystalline structure that rises to 150 feet and stretches for more than a mile along the river. In addition, the Rock of the Raven represents the dividing line between the Carolina Piedmont and Coastal Plain. Siouan and Tuscarora Indians hunted the area until the mid-1700s, and many arrowheads and pottery fragments have been discovered in the vicinity.

The best whitewater of the river (yes there are rapids in the western coastal plain), can be found in section three. Begin at the SR 2016 access and paddle through the ledges until you reach the NC 217 bridge in Erwin. The rapids are largely the result of a major flood in 1865, which washed away several rock-filled wooden dams and locks that had been built by the Cape Fear Navigation Company. Their remains, together with a gradient that drops about 12 feet per mile, can be challenging to a novice paddler, so use caution. This paddle will take you in the area of a legitimate ghost town, that being Averasboro, once the third-largest village in colonial North Carolina. Approximately 3 miles southwest of Dunn you will find the Averasboro Battleground, where Confederate General Hardee clashed with Gen. Sherman's left flank as a precursor to Bentonville. A new railroad came to the area in the 1880s, by-passing Averasboro but going directly through the heart of nearby Dunn. Such was the beginning of the end for a once flourishing little town.

These are but a few of the southeastern area paddling voyages that our state has to offer, but each is unique in their inherent combination of accessibility and coastal plain/ eastern piedmont wilderness. The majority can be considered suitable for a short family day trip, yet offer the option of more lengthy exploration. Hence, they qualify for author's choice, but are not exclusive in that other similar bodies of water exist within the area that can become "reader's choice." I would encourage you to look at the Black River, the Lumbee, and other points along the Cape Fear River for more variety of experiences within this region.

Approaching the Great Smoky Mountains National Park
at Fontana Lake

Chapter Three:

The Land of the Sky

*"...the river, always the river, the dark eternal
river, full of strange secret time, washing the
city's stains away...is flowing by us, by us,
to the sea."*

—*Thomas Wolfe*

No writer can match the eloquent command that Asheville's native son maintained over the English language. Most certainly the former quote references the predominant river of the mountain region, our own French Broad, which was to Wolfe as the Mississippi was to a guy named Sam Clemens. But before we reach what was deemed *Acgiqua (Long Man)* by the native Cherokee, we must first make our way westward in the footsteps of a legendary pioneer.

A.   Paddling in Boone's Backyard

Although he will best be remembered for his frontier epic encounters and his Kentucky rifle, if Daniel Boone had not followed the Yadkin River upstream then who knows when Cumberland Gap might have been discovered? Boone came south from Pennsylvania with his family when his father Squire secured a warrant that claimed 640 acres in an area known as Forks of the Yadkin back in the fall of 1750. Some locals say that the Boones lived in a cave on the east side of the Yadkin during their first few months before building a cabin along Lickon Creek in present-day Davie County. It is remarkable to paddle past Boone's Cave State Park and climb the wooden staircase up from the river to the cave, which is approximately 80 feet long and very narrow. At the top you will also find a gravestone inscribed "Boone", but it is uncertain just which pioneer relative was laid to rest within the park. Legend also has it that Daniel himself used the cave as a hideout from the *Yattken* Indians, a small Siouan tribe that inhabited the foothills. A probable relative of the Catawba, the name translates into *"place of big trees."*

Yet another tale insists that nearby Bear Creek was named from the season that Boone killed ninety-nine bears along its waters. This scenic creek, which is slightly southeast of the Uwharries in Moore County and close to the pottery capital of Seagrove, offers a nice paddle of about 2 miles. A favorite access point lies at the end of Carter's Mill Road just north of Robbins, and take-out just before the remains of historic Reynolds Mill *(built by the father of Judge Rufus W. Reynolds, North Carolina's first federal bankruptcy judge)*. An alternate put-in at the NC 705 bridge in Robbins will add about a mile to the trip, which takes you through an area of little development and abandoned mill sites.

If you have time, visit the "House in the Horseshoe" a few miles to the east near Sanford, home of former Governor Tom Benjamin Williams (1751-1814). The colonial home, built in 1770 by Philip Alston, is one of but a few remaining structures in the nation where you can see actual bullet holes from a Revolutionary War skirmish. On July 29, 1781, British loyalists led by Commander David Fanning attacked Alston and his band of Patriots. Alston was forced to surrender after the British attempted to set fire to his home with a cart of burning straw. Williams, who served under George Washington in the 2nd N.C. Continental Regiment, bought the home in 1798 prior to his initial election as governor the following year. He served in that capacity from 1799-1802, and again from 1807-1808.

Yadkin area access can be found off of NC 801 just north of Salisbury, and a paddle downstream to High Rock Lake will take you by Boone's Cave approximately 2 miles from the put-in. High Rock offers nice views of the Unwharrie Mountains to the east, and a mid-week trip should avoid significant boat traffic. An optional put-in can be found at the wildlife access area in Southmont, about 15 miles south of Lexington off of NC 8, and you can venture towards Abbott's Creek and explore several small islands full of rocks for skipping. The mouth of the creek lies on the opposite shore from the access, and crossing is only about a mile from your point of embark. High Rock is likewise convenient to the Salisbury area, and additional wildlife access points can be found along the western shore. The lake offers an easy, flat-water respite that borders game lands and mature forest.

A short jaunt downstream takes us into the Uwharrie National Forest, an oasis within the western piedmont region. There we find Badin Lake, another man-made creation from the legendary Yadkin which serves as a cousin to High Rock Lake. The Uwharries represent perhaps the oldest "mountain" range in the country, although some may consider them to be more in the nature of foothills. Rising to almost 2,000 feet above sea level, they give the appearance of being at a seemingly higher elevation since the valleys fall far below. As a comparison, the City of Asheville was built on a valley floor with an elevation of approximately 2,300. Although the 50,189 acres of the Uwharrie National Forest make it the smallest national forest in North Carolina, the forest service contends that it offers more archeological sites per acre than any other in the southeastern United States.

Even the legendary John Lawson , the same original resident of Bath Town who sailed to the Carolina Coast in August of 1700, has ties to this region. He decided to venture into the unknown and potentially hostile back-country by canoe with an Indian guide, as little was known of the Native American inhabitants of the area. In late January 1701, Lawson and his entourage of five Englishmen and various Indian guides crossed into

North Carolina in the neighborhood of present-day Charlotte, then the land of the Catawba. Continuing a northerly trek, on February 5, 1702, his party crossed the Uwharrie River (recorded as "Heighwaree" by Lawson) and came upon the village of Keyauwee Town.

If you wish to follow the Lawson route, access areas for Badin Lake can be found in both Montgomery and Stanley counties. Morrow Mountain State Park lies just to the southwest of the impoundment, creating a corridor of forest on both sides of what is now called the Pee Dee River. For some reason, the Yadkin changes its name when it leaves the Badin Dam, but keep going south and you will reach the third cousin in the chain of lakes, that being Lake Tillery. Access areas are offered on both the eastern and western shorelines, and it is easy to find the private nooks and crannies that only the paddler can appreciate.

Keep in mind that Boone's Yadkin (aka Pee Dee) is the connector from High Rock to Tillery, and that wildlife access areas are easy to be located at points in between. A trip to Troy, Albemarle, or Mt. Gilead would be a convenient base for selected day trips on the water. Mt. Gilead features the *Town Creek Indian Mound* just east of town, which offers a glimpse into an excavated pre-Columbian settlement along Little River. Artifacts found in the area date back to the eleventh century.

While the Pee Dee continues its journey into South Carolina and on to the Atlantic Ocean, our epic pioneer (Mr. Boone that is) gained fame from going the opposite direction in an unconventional manner known as "poling." Poling what was likely a poplar dugout upstream against the current all the way to the headwaters of the Yadkin near present-day Blowing Rock must have been a grueling experience. No doubt he traveled through one of his namesake towns known now as Boonville, and skirted the Mt. Airy hometown of Andy Griffith. He may have camped at nearby Pilot Mountain, known as "Mount Pilot" to Mayberry residents. The latter areas are considered part of the Sauratown Mountain Range, slightly larger than the Uwharries yet smaller than the Appalachians. Although Myers Lake only exists within the creative minds of the television series, a nearby paddle along a neighboring river is worth a side trip.

The river of reference is the Dan, another topographical tribute to the infamous pioneer, and can be found about a half-hour's drive to the north of Winston-Salem. Hanging Rock State Park in Stokes County offers public access to the Dan River, and it is approximately five and a half miles from the park to take out at Moratock Park Access near Danbury. This stretch features high rocky bluffs and caves to explore with a "mountain feel" and clear water. You would never guess that the triad metro was nearby. Other access points can be found at the 704 bridge, the NC 89 bridge, and the Hemlock golf course, which enables the paddler to tackle up to 27 miles of river depending upon his or her allotted time frame.

A final Yadkin River paddle to consider would be the stretch from the Grandin Road bridge in Caldwell County to the end of Wilkes County Rt. 1137 on Kerr Scott Lake, a distance of approximately nine miles. Another Boone family home was located nearby on the tributary of Beaver Creek, about three-fourths of a mile north of the river. Unless you wish to drag your boat under a draping canopy of forested tree limbs, I would not suggest any attempt to venture up Beaver Creek. You can shorten the Grandin to Kerr voyage to about five miles by putting in at the bridge in Ferguson. Since the Yadkin ends, or rather begins, prior to reaching the bustling town of Boone, we must switch gears and adjust paddles to yet another river of colonial and pioneer legacy: the New.

It must have been somewhat ironic to Peter Jefferson, the father of Thomas, that what he would call the New River is actually thought to be the world's second oldest river after the Nile. Peter, who visited the area as a surveyor in 1749, is credited with having given the New its current name. The New is predominantly shallow and mild, very conducive to a family paddle, and originates in Ashe County near the Virginia border. A 26 mile stretch that includes sections in both states makes for a quality overnighter with a stop at New River State Park (featuring paddle-in campsites), but other opportunities for day trips abound.

A favorite trek from years back begins at the NC 1560 bridge northeast of Boone near the community of Todd. Put-in is actually on the South Fork of the New, but the river merges with the North Fork northeast of Jefferson just past Twin Rivers Campground. You will pass the state park during this voyage of approximately 9 miles to Mouth of Wilson, VA, with signs clearly visible from the water. It is not uncommon to startle whitetail deer along the shoreline of this relatively undeveloped region. The community of Todd features a "throwback" general store that deserves a visit, and several outfitters operate in the area should you desire to customize your journey and maximize your time.

Another paddle of note along the South Fork begins at the US 221 bridge, which is not an optimum access point but leads to a tranquil paddle with two low-water bridges between the put-in and take out at NC 1179. You could also continue to the NC 163 bridge for take-out, but that adds 9.5 miles to what is otherwise an approximate 5 mile paddle. The rainbow trout were hitting on spinnerbaits back in 1992, and beaver were encountered both then and in 1994 which I regret to say was the last official visit by the author to date. It's past time to get reacquainted and bring the fishing rod! Smallmouth and "redeye" bass also await the angling paddler.

Many other options for day trips can be found along the New, and trip information can be easily obtained from local outfitters in the vicinity of Jefferson. Several private campsites are located riverside in places such as Glendale Springs, Piney Creek, Crumpler and West Jefferson, awaiting exploration by adventuresome families.

Time to shift gears and offer a footnote to the Central Piedmont, otherwise defined as the triangle to the east (Raleigh/Durham/Chapel Hill), the triad (Greensboro/Winston-Salem/High Point) to the south, and Charlotte Metro to the southwest. This area is host to approximately eighty percent of our state's populous, but does offer a quadrant of paddling turf worthy of mention. To be fair, this author has spent more time in search of wilderness waterways elsewhere in the Old North State, but on occasion has discovered some voyages of respite from the hustle and bustle that typifies the metro region.

One such paddle worthy of inclusion would be Mountain Island Lake. This small gem of the piedmont is an impoundment of the Catawba River, located approximately 5 miles south of busy Lake Norman.

Canoe access points are located in Latta Plantation Park in Mecklenburg County, home to the Carolina Raptor Center, which features everything from rehabilitating bald eagles to owls and turkey vultures. Located less than 30 minutes from the Queen City, Latta serves as a tranquil measure of escape from the urban entrapment of Charlotte metropolis. Gar Creek access is on the left near the end of Sample Road just past the Raptor Center, and North Shore access can be found with a right turn off of Sample Road just prior to the Center.

Within the plantation park you will still find a good deal of undeveloped shoreline with an occasional Osprey nest. Many trails cross through the mature woodlands, and whitetail deer are often encountered. Mountain Island itself is uninhabited and less than a one mile paddle from the North Shore put-in. A great spot for the young paddlers to dinosaur hunt!

While in the Charlotte area, don't miss the U.S. National Whitewater Center (city folk do enjoy a few spoils every now and then!). You can marvel as Olympic hopefuls tackle the artificial whitewater, or drop your own paddle at the Catawba River access point near the South Trail. With over 1.5 miles of river frontage along the Catawba, the Center provides excellent opportunities for paddlers of all skill levels. Long Creek serves as the northern boundary of the Center and is easy to explore by kayak or canoe. In addition, the South Fork River is only a short paddle from the Catawba Access and features numerous tributary creeks accessible only via canoe or kayak.

Although you can't paddle to it, colonial history buffs should take time to visit the *Rock House* while in the vicinity of our Queen City (3500 Shamrock Drive in the eastern section of town). The former home of Hezekiah Alexander, who supervised the raising, provisioning, and financing of area Patriot forces during the American Revolution, is among the few remaining pre-revolutionary structures in the piedmont. It may also be the oldest free-standing, documented Masonic structure in the nation.

During the first few weeks of May, 1775, news of the fighting between the British and Massachusetts "minutemen" at Lexington and Concord spread throughout North Carolina. On May 20, 1775, the people of Mecklenburg County responded by declaring themselves to be a free and independent people. Eleven days later, the Mecklenburg County Committee of Safety met and agreed upon the *Mecklenburg Resolves*, endorsed by Alexander and others, which essentially declared English law to be invalid. After all, since Parliament had declared America to be in a state of rebellion, laws and commissions that derived their authority from England should thereby carry no legal weight. Such set the stage for the July 4, 1776, approval of Thomas Jefferson's Declaration of Independence by the Continental Congress in Philadelphia.

Time to return to the Catawba, which is the namesake of yet another historical Native American tribe, originally known as *Iswa, "the river people."* During the time of Hezekiah, as many as 5,000 tribal members lived along the river banks near what was then known as Charlotteown. In contrast to the approach taken by many original inhabitants, the Catawba became fast allies with the colonial English, even joining them against the French, Cherokee, and others during the French and Indian War. North of Lake Norman, in the Hickory and Morganton areas, many additional Catawba River access points can be found to allow for trips of varying duration.

The Catawba River Basin begins on the eastern slopes of the McDowell County mountains and flows southeast through North Carolina until reaching the state border at Lake Wylie. The 224 mile river includes a chain of seven man-made lakes, and its longest free-flowing stretch covers only about 17 miles. Although perhaps the most densely populated basin within the state, the upper reaches of this history laden river are still quite pristine.

At Quaker Meadows near Morganton, the mountain men responsible for the American Revolutionary War victory at Kings Mountain camped along the banks of the Catawba, a mere 7 days before the epic battle that served as a turning point in the war. On October 7, 1780, after riding all night and fording the swollen Broad River, the mountaineers with their long rifles either killed or captured the entire Loyalist army in less than an hour. This victory is widely regarded as a key turning point for America's fortunes in the war, which ended a mere 12 months and 12 days later when Cornwallis surrendered to Washington at Yorktown.

Before we continue our trek west, both Lake James and the South Fork of the Catawba offer options for paddling excursions. In McDowell County just off of interstate 40 lies what is considered by many to be the first significant "mountain country" lake. Many will remember James Fenimore Cooper's frontier saga known as the *Last of the Mohicans*, and a significant number of scenes from the movie were filmed in and around Lake James. On the Linville side of the lake, near where the fort was constructed for the film, the North Fork Access area showcases beautiful vistas of Hawksbill, Table Rock, Shortoff, and Brown Mountain. The latter is known as being home to the mysterious Brown Mountain Lights, which have intrigued visitors for centuries. Keep an eye peeled toward the northeast Blue Ridge and watch for what some describe as a glowing ball of fire.

The lights date back to Native American mythology as early as the year 1200. According to Cherokee legend, a great battle between the Cherokee and Catawba occurred at that time, and the lights represent the spirits of Indian maidens who continue to search through the centuries for those slain in the ancient battle. Other legendary accounts include that of the slave who continues to search for his planter/owner from the low country who became lost while hunting. Yet another involves a woman who was allegedly murdered by her husband back in 1850, and her ghost continues to haunt the mountain to this day. It has been confirmed that years later, a skeleton of the missing woman was found under a cliff along the mountainside!

The "first" lost colony of North Carolina is also found within the Upper Catawba River Valley. Lesser known than its English cousin to the east, Spanish conquistador Juan Pardo built Fort San Juan at a location along Upper Creek near the ancestral river town of Joara. The year was 1567, predating the Roanoke Island colony by two decades. Fort San Juan thereby enjoys the designation of being the earliest European settlement in the interior of what is now the United States. Fast forward to 1568, when only one Spanish survivor was left to attest that the fort had been overrun by the Catawba and burned to the ground. Now known as the Berry site, archaeologists from Warren Wilson College are continuing to excavate and uncover the mysteries of this lost colony.

Not far from Upper Creek, the Linville River enters Lake James after leaving the gorge which also bears its name (actually, pioneer William Linville and his sons were scalped in 1766 while exploring the area, but their legacy lives on perpetually through the namesake river and gorge). Linville River, however, represents more of a fishing as opposed to paddling option at this point. In this section of the modern-day frontier, Lake James is the place to put-in as it is quite amenable to the shoreline paddler. Consider a voyage to the mouth of the Linville, but remember to bring the rod and reel. On the east end of the lake, the Catawba's south fork enters and allows for ideal family paddling both upstream and down. Both private and public access areas are easily found near Marion. Take NC 226 north and take a right on Hankins Road. After only a couple of miles, the lake will appear on the horizon.

Back to Morganton and the 21st century we go, and do consider a paddle on the Johns River just north of town. A relatively unknown, yet easy to paddle river, the Johns originates in the Pisgah National Forest and drains Wilson's Creek, known to be a world-class trout stream. Put-in off NC 18/US 64, and you have about 1.5 miles to paddle downstream before confluence with the Catawba. If you continue, you will soon enter the impoundment of Lake Rhodhiss. Along the way you will experience a wilderness environment with many spots to fish or picnic.

B.   The Blue Ridge and Beyond

It seems befitting to conclude this paddle through history in the geographic area where the majority of my adult life has been spent, a region filled with whitewater rivers and pristine, blue-water lakes. The naturalist William Bartram befittingly described the area as being where one can behold a *"world of mountains piled upon mountains."* Native American origins can be traced archaeologically back to the Paleo-Indian nomadic period of 10,000-8,000 B.C., and throughout the centuries native cultures have relied upon the poplar dugout canoe to traverse the waterways of their ancestral Appalachians. Unlike Northeastern and Canadian tribes, the Cherokee did not have access to the numerous white birch trees that dominate the boreal northern forests. Thus, as opposed to the more nimble and light-weight birchbark canoe, the Southern Appalachians gave birth to the poplar dugout, a close cousin of the cypress dugouts from eastern North Carolina. At the Oconaluftee Indian Village on the Cherokee Reservation, you can observe the process of how native artisans re-create the dugout canoe.

It is amazing to consider that in 1735 the Cherokee inhabited approximately 40,000 square miles, with 64 towns and villages in the mountain region. They called the area "Sha-Kon-O-Hey", the phonetic spelling for "Land of Blue Smoke." There are many varieties of family friendly adventures to be discovered in this wilderness paradise, from pristine flat water lakes to fast moving whitewater rivers. If a dugout isn't handy, canoes or kayaks with a keel or shallow "v" hull configuration would be the best choice for the former. These are generally made of wood, fiberglass, or aluminum. Whereas virtually any material can be used for flat water, whitewater requires a construction design that will not crack or puncture. Without going into a detailed description of the many varieties of composites that are available, suffice it to say that some form of ABS plastic construction should suffice.

Imagine yourself by the lake at dawn, that gray area between night and day when fog clings to the water and invokes a surreal aura amid the world waking around it. So what are you waiting for? Let's begin with a section of Jackson County known locally as "Little Canada." I'm not certain of the exact source that designated the area as such, but the area bears a striking resemblance to prototypical Canadian wilderness waterways. A total of four lakes connect the Tuckasegee River, with each impoundment featuring a unique paddling experience. Each lake was created on the east fork of the river back in the mid 1950s in an effort to provide hydroelectric power to the region.

Cedar Cliff Lake represents the first in the chain if you are moving from west to east, and is the most accessible by automobile. From Sylva, take NC 107 south a little over ten miles to the community of Tuckasegee. Take the next left on Shook Cove Road (SR 1135), which is just past the left on NC 281 (*281 takes you to the remaining three lakes), and Cedar Cliff will appear within minutes. There is a wildlife put-in that you can't miss, and a waterfall on the eastern edge of the lake which serves as the boundary to Bear Lake. The Tuckasegee River emerges from the western edge of Cedar Cliff, and offers yet another paddling option with several access points along 107 as you head downstream to Cullowhee.

Bear Lake is first in line to reach if you take the 281 option, and represents the largest body of water in the chain, covering almost 500 acres. As the big brother of the group, it also has a greater degree of development and boat traffic. Accordingly, this author recommends that you continue on to next door Wolf Creek Lake, or further to the smallest impoundment known as Tanasee Creek Lake. Wolf Creek is approximately three miles long and is a paddlers dream, with surrounding Pisgah National Forest and many tranquil spots to beach the boat. Tanasee is a miniature bookend of only about a mile in length, but rarely will you find much additional company on the water. Both Wolf Creek and Tanasee offer great summer cool water swimming, and quiet fall leaf-season colors while the cars are bumper-to-bumper on the Blue Ridge Parkway.

In the Little Canada community known as East LaPorte, also just off of NC 107 and about a mile from the 281 turnoff, you will find a most curious artifact of Native American lore known as the Judaculla Rock. This soapstone boulder is covered in petroglyphs, and can be reached via SR 1737, also known as Caney Fork Road. Locals say the rock bears the handprint of the Cherokee giant Judaculla, who could drink a stream dry with one gulp and used lightening as arrows for his immortal bow. The slant-eyed giant allegedly leaped down off a nearby mountain and scratched the rock with his seven-fingered hands. Archaeological excavations in the vicinity have revealed, among other finds, stone bowls and quarrying tools dating back to the Late Archaic Period of 3000-1000 B.C.

Continue south on 107 and the road begins to rise. Higher and higher you climb and all of a sudden the blue water of Lake Glenville (aka Thorpe Reservoir) appears with a shoreline elevation of approximately 3,800 feet. Considered to be the highest major lake in eastern America, Glenville is six miles long with 26 miles of frequently sandy shores to explore. A mixture of Pisgah National Forest and areas of development surround the lake, which features many islands and coves to discover. Peregrine Falcons roost on Whiteside Mountain, easily seen from the lake, where the mythical *Utlunta ("spear finger")* of Cherokee lore attempted to build a great rock bridge through the air to Hiwassee. His efforts were said to be thwarted by lightening, yet locals insist that remnants of the bridge can still be seen on Whiteside.

Since we can't utilize *Utlunta's* byway, our trek west must continue by road to a little known lake which feeds an infamous river—the Nantahala. Just south of the gorge, the lake is somewhat secluded with Nantahala National Forest on the western shore and limited development to the east. A few miles east of Andrews, it can be accessed from SR 1310 from the east and SR 1401 to the west (access via the adjoining forest service road). Bear hunting is prevalent within this area of national forest, so be aware and check your calendar for timing. One November many years ago we encountered a frightened raccoon swimming towards our canoe while attempting to escape from the barking blue tick coonhounds that it had left behind on the shore.

If you are in the mood for whitewater thrills, leave the lake and continue north into the "Land of the Noonday Sun" gorge and visit one of the area outfitters for a river run. The Nantahala Outdoor Center is a world-renowned training ground for Olympic paddlers, many of whom can be observed on any given day practicing on the river. For those who would rather stick to flat-water,

Lake Santeelah is a short hop, skip, and jump to the northwest.

Santeelah is located off of US 129 in Graham County, just next to Robbinsville, a picturesque little town perhaps best known as a filming location for Jodie Foster's movie *Nell*. Chief Junaluska, the Cherokee hero credited with saving the life of Andrew Jackson at the Battle of Horeshoe Bend, is interred in the local cemetery. Ironically, Jackson later betrayed the Cherokee when he sanctioned Indian removal in 1838, a dark era for American history that came to be known as the *Trail of Tears*. Although Junaluska was forced to join his comrades in the march to Oklahoma, he returned to North Carolina on foot and in 1847 was awarded land in the Robbinsville vicinity. Together with Colonel William Thomas, he is credited with being primarily responsible for the recognition of the Cherokee Eastern Band. He died in 1868 at the ripe old age of 93.

Popular with paddlers, the lower section of Santeelah towards the Horse Cove camping area and Little Santeelah Creek avoids most of the motorboat traffic that can be found near Cheoah Point above the dam. There are many secluded spots to investigate, and the Snowbird Mountains to the South and Unicoi to the west foster an elegant alpine curtain that is difficult to reduce to a written description.

Although you can't paddle to it, when in the Santeelah area be sure to take the short drive to Joyce Kilmer Memorial Forest. From the lake, simply continue on SR 416 after passing Horse Cove and you will soon reach the picnic area. Set aside in 1936 as a living memorial to the poet/soldier Kilmer, this forest is the most impressive example of original, old-growth in the eastern United

States. An easy 2-mile loop trail winds through the towering trees, many of whom are over 100 feet tall and over 20 feet in circumference. At many spots on the forest floor you can see remnants of the massive American Chestnut trees that dominated the forest prior to the blight which began in 1925. When the earth was created, the abundant Frazier Fir and Hemlock were among the species that did not fall asleep. Accordingly, they remain evergreen year round. Even now, this virgin wilderness remains a place of inspiration and a treasure of native flora and fauna.

Canoe "purists" will always rave, and justifiably so, about the Boundary Waters Wilderness of the Minnesota/Canadian border. North Carolina, however, can also boast of its own boundary water—that being Calderwood Reservoir which straddles the Swain County and Blount County, Tennessee line. Put in at Tapoco just off 129 and below the Cheoah Dam, and a paddle west will take you into Davey Crockett country in about a mile. What begins as Nantahala National Forest turns into Cherokee National Forest, with more isolation and remote wilderness than you will find just about anywhere else within the region. Several small waterfalls appear on the north shore of the lake as you paddle towards Slickrock Creek, the mouth of which lies just into the Tennessee side on the southern shore. The creek is navigable only for about a hundred yards, but a hiking trail runs alongside it and allows for a nice interlude to stretch your legs.

Calderwood is a short jaunt west from Fontana Lake (see discussion below) and north of Santeelah, and one would be remiss to bypass the splendor it offers when paddling within the area. Cheoah Reservoir adjoins Calderwood to the east and is likewise a popular paddling destination. Follow NC 28 west from Fontana and you will arrive at Cheoah in approximately 5 miles.

The Little Tennessee River, perhaps the most environmentally healthy river in the mountain region, enters Fontana on the south side after flowing through alternating farmlands and woodlands in both Macon and Swain counties. Rock hounds love the town of Franklin, formerly known as *Nikwasi* to the Cherokee, which is widely renowned for its gem mining and mineral deposits. Take advantage of a calm paddle that winds through the town courtesy of a local greenway, or venture beyond into mild whitewater that leads past the site of the ancient Cherokee town of *Cowee ("wolf-clan place")*.

If the former appeals to you, put in at Big Bear Park located on Northeast Main Street, where you will also find picnic shelters and a playground for the kids. The 1540 De Soto expedition crossed the Little Tennessee in this area, and it is approximately a 3 mile paddle along the greenway to the Nonah Bridge just off the US 64 Bypass/US 441 overpass. An alternative route with a genuine wilderness feel would be to put in at the NC 28 bridge at Iotla for a ten mile run to Lost Bridge. It's not hard to locate a grassy bank suitable for canoe camping along this stretch if you wish to break up the trip. Cowee was located in this vicinity, and visible evidence of ancient fish weirs can be seen just north of town where the river rejoins NC 28. Both the Cherokee and the frontier pioneers would herd fish through the open end of the "V" rock structures into waiting nets, which was less challenging than the fly rod but likely more productive!

An additional 13 miles brings you to Fontana Lake, however this section of river can be quite difficult, especially when lake levels are low. My advice would be to utilize the roof racks on your canoe-mobile and drive to the US 19 bridge just southwest of Bryson City. A flat-water paddle can begin here, or at backwater access areas where either the Nantahala or Tuckasegee Rivers enter the lake. A favorite put in lies within the *Tsali* Recreation Area, known for its premier mountain bike trails, but on the campground side. Put in on Mouse Branch Creek and you'll reach the main body of the lake in about a mile and a half. The Great Smoky Mountains National Park dominates the north shore of Fontana, while the Nanta-hala National Forest covers much of the southern shore.

Tsali ("Charlie"), represents more than just the name of a canoe station, and his legend remains an inspi-ration to the Cherokee people. Under the terms of the 1836 Treaty of New Echota, all Cherokee were required to give up their homeland and move to the west of the Mississippi River. Tsali, who had not been privy to the treaty process, was living at the time with his wife and three children in a cabin near the mouth of the Nantahala River. Soldiers arrived at his home during the summer of 1838, evicted the family and marched them towards Bushnell Stockade (now covered by the waters of Fontana). Accounts differ as to how and why, but all agree that an altercation occurred while en route to the stockade, resulting in the death of at least one soldier.

Tsali escaped and a manhunt ensued, resulting in the eventual capture and execution of several Cherokee. Tsali's wife and youngest son were spared, but a total of four, including Tsali, were tied to a tree and shot. It was widely reported that Tsali had surrendered so that federal troops would leave his beloved mountains and allow his kinsmen, many of whom were hiding in area caves and "hollars", to remain in their homeland. No doubt the spirits of these heroic men still wander the shores of Fontana. Without such sacrifice, it is likely that the stage would never have been set for recognition of the Eastern Band of Cherokee.

Perhaps the most beautiful lake east of the Mississippi, Fontana has 240 miles of shoreline and covers over 10,500 acres. Dam construction began in 1942, and in 1944 the lake began to fill. The entire town of Judson was submerged, and many valley homes and farms were flooded. Accordingly, the ghosts of pioneers past are said to be seen alongside the artifacts of their existence, forever lost and wandering the deep waters.

Many access areas can be found along the lakeshore, from Alarka on the east to Fontana Village on the western edge, but be cognizant of the motorboat traffic that will likely share in at least the beginning of your journey. A personal favorite somewhat off the grid is the Wilderness access area in the Roundhill Community just west of Bryson City. From there it is about a two mile paddle to the mouth of Forney Creek along the north shore, which is a great spot for a picnic, hike, or overnight canoe camp.

This area of the national park is quite remote, and we have often seen tracks of the park's signature mammal, the black bear *("Yanegwa" in Cherokee)*, while exploring the creek bed. Several years ago we even spotted a bear relocation cage a few yards off the trail! Bears, like their brethren alligator to the east, are the kings of their environment but generally afraid of humans. An occasional attack within the region is reported, so take necessary precautions, but don't let unwarranted phobia keep you away from the jewel that is Fontana Lake.

C.   Tahkeyostee and the Nunnehi

There was a time when people came to the mountains to breathe the fresh air, enjoy the spectacular scenery, and experience a lifestyle quite the opposite from that which they had grown accustomed. Today, although development has had its impact, there is still a place where mountain breezes blow unfettered through the trees, and where one of the most historic rivers still flows as it always has, through forest, field and mountain valley. That would be the French Broad, one of several places where the mythical world of the mountains still comes alive.

Native American legend has it that the *Nunnehi*, a race of immortal spirits, inhabit rock caves along the river. They are the "little people", hardly reaching up to a man's knee in height, but well-shaped and handsome with long hair flowing almost to the ground. They are charged with protecting the French Broad and other mountain rivers from those who would bring harm to the ecosystem. No doubt that Iron Eyes Cody has summoned their assistance during his lifelong battle against pollution.

The French Broad will be forever memorialized in the treatise of the same name written by the late Wilma Dykeman, and first published in 1955. This author would be doing the reader a disservice by attempting to provide a comparable history, when such a comprehensive account is still in print and readily available. Consequently, we will focus on the many sections of the river that offer the modern day pioneer a variety of 21st century wilderness encounters.

Acgiqua carves its way through the rugged slopes of some of the earth's oldest mountains, winding a total of 117 miles through North Carolina's share of the Appalachians. Hernando De Soto's expedition passed through the area in 1540 while searching for gold, and there remains today a legend of a cave laden with silver that overlooks the river at Hot Springs. If you take out or put in at Hot Springs, be sure to hike the Silvermine Trail up to Lover's Leap and take a dip in the natural mineral hot tubs upon return (see additional discussion later in the chapter).

Early European settlers bestowed upon the river its current name, largely because it flowed northwest into what was then French territory. In the 1780s, the first English settlers crossed the Blue Ridge, with Samuel Davidson settling above the Swannanoa River, a tributary of the French Broad that is likewise navigable by canoe when water levels are up. Davidson was reportedly killed by a Native American hunting party, and his grave lies just off a Warren Wilson College trail near the Swannanoa. The Swannanoa can be accessed at the college, only a few miles from US 70 east of Asheville. From there to Recreation Park in Asheville the paddle is about 11 miles through what are largely wooded areas and farmland. If you take out at the US 70 bridge at Azalea, the trip can be shortened to about 8 miles.

The Swannanoa, a "chattering child of the Long Man", flows into the French Broad just south of downtown after a run through both metro areas and Biltmore Estate property. The Biltmore Avenue bridge in South Asheville can be a makeshift access option to avoid the former, and allows for a forested 2.5 mile paddle to Jean Webb Park on the French Broad. Keep in mind that the Swannanoa is a narrow stream with many downed trees ("strainers"), and susceptible to water level impediments. The best time for paddling is generally the spring, especially when the dogwoods begin to bloom.

From Champion Park near its headwaters in Rosman, to Hominy Creek Park in Asheville, the French Broad has been designated a North Carolina River Trail. This was the first such designation by our state. Generally a placid, flat-water stream south of Asheville, the river changes character after leaving the big city. Whitewater, both mild and that worthy of portage, begins to coincide with the paddler's exit from the metro area. The Cherokee called this section of the river *"Tahkeyostee" ("where they race"),* and many outfitters offer rafting trips along the Class III to V rapids of section 9 in Madison County.

For family-oriented solace and calm water, begin near the upstream terminus. Try the put-in at Champion Park in Rosman, just off NC 64 along Old Rosman Road. It is a mere 2.5 miles to the access at Lyon's Mountain Road, and another 5 miles to the kind folks at Headwaters Outfitters. Island Ford Road access is yet another 2 miles, so many take-out options exist. This section represents the beginning of the "Long Man", as the East, West, and North Forks of the river all merge together in Rosman. The river is quite narrow through this stretch as it meanders through farm country with an occasional long range mountain view.

Another familiar run begins at Island Ford in Transylvania County (yes, potential vampires most certainly do abound, especially given that the landmark monolith known as Devil's Courthouse is nearby along the Blue Ridge Parkway). From Island Ford to Hap Simpson Park in Brevard the paddle is approximately 8 miles of a largely calm and winding channel, but one never knows what adventure lies around the next bend. The site of the Island Ford access marks a historical pioneer crossing, and pieces of old wagons are sometimes seen when the river is low.

The following war story has to be worthy of inclusion. During the late '90s on a warm spring day, our family of four decided to explore the aforementioned section of river for the first time. I'm taking a break from paddling, having turned it over to the kids (ages 10 and 8 at the time), and had just cracked open a Bud light. All of a sudden I hear farmer Wilson yelling at us. "Come here, I need your help!" he bellowed towards our approaching vessel. "Excuse me?" was all I could muster. For all I knew, he could have been the father of Eric Rudolph or possibly some relative of the Deliverance movie cast.

"My cow is giving birth and the calf is breached." Well, that ruled out Rudolph and the enemies of Burt Reynolds, but it was my grandparents and not I that had grown up on a farm. Turns out that farmer Wilson needed help to insert the rope around the calf, then pull it out. If not, no doubt both mother and baby wouldn't make it.

To shorten the tale, both myself and our wide-eyed kids watched as my wife (a people nurse, not a vet), inserted the rope and tied it off. After that enlightening educational experience, Mr. Wilson and I were able to yank out baby Bessie. We visited for a time, said our goodbyes, and continued on our journey. No vampires or dinosaurs, but definitely a trip that will be remembered by all.

The Transylvania region is known as the "land of the waterfalls", and features the Estatoe Trail, a Cherokee "highway" that linked mountain settlements with the town of the same name in South Carolina. The trail crossed the state line near Rosman, and passed through the county seat of Brevard. Near the Hannah's Ford access, at a place called Bunker Hill, a skirmish is said to have been fought in 1811. This was part of an ongoing land dispute between both Carolinas and Georgia, and was known as the Walton War. At some point John Boy apparently said good night and the boundaries were settled.

The French Broad continues its northwesterly flow downstream from Transylvania into Henderson County, then veers to the east for several miles. The river is still bordered largely by agricultural bottom land, with the first river access being at Blantyre, found off of SR 1503 and just a short distance from US Hwy 64. It is about 10.5 river miles to the first take-out at Johnson Bridge off Banner Farm Road, and another 2 miles to Kings Road access on NC 191. From Kings Road, Westfeldt River Park is an approximate 6 mile paddle.

Another stretch of flat-water takes us from Henderson County to Buncombe, with access points beginning at Glenn Bridge River Park, also off of 191 and about 2 miles from Westfeldt. After reaching Glenn Bridge, the river runs parallel to Interstate 26 for most of its 5.5 mile trek to Bent Creek River Park , just next to the Blue Ridge Parkway and the North Carolina Arboretum. Additional access points can be found at Hominy Creek, French Broad River Park, and Jean Webb Park in the heart of Asheville's river district.

The Bent Creek to Hominy paddle of approximately 6 miles takes you by George Vanderbilt's stunning mansion, the Biltmore House, which is America's largest privately owned residence. Vanderbilt (1862-1914), purchased approximately 125,000 acres of wilderness and constructed his palace on land that remains in the hands of his heirs to this day. In lieu of developing the remaining acreage, the family donated the majority of his property to create modern-day Pisgah National Forest. Be prepared for some company on this segment of the voyage, however, unless you pick the right time of day. Riverlink of Asheville offers a wonderful map that provides detailed access information about all of these and other French Broad options, and I highly recommend it as a handy guide.

North of Asheville, above the dam in Woodfin, the waters of *Tahkeyostee* begin as the personality of the river begins its transformation. The little town of Woodfin has recently opened a river park next to NC 251, otherwise known as "river road." While located within a fairly developed district, it is possible to put-in here and paddle upstream for some smallmouth or muskie fishing. If you choose to venture downstream, however, be ready for some consistent Class III level whitewater. Ledges Whitewater Park is approximately 3.5 miles from Woodfin, with Walnut Island Park another 5 miles.

Although the river snakes its way between 251 and the Norfolk-Southern railroad, the municipal flavor of Jean Webb and Woodfin soon give way to a wilderness feel. As many bicycles as vehicles enjoy the scenic road, which hugs the rocky cliffs of the French Broad River Gorge all the way to Marshall. Those motorists in a hurry generally take the 4-lane highway that runs parallel on the opposite side of the gorge, so the sounds of the river frequently sing solo. NC 251 was once part of the infamous Buncombe Turnpike, the principal thoroughfare for trade between South Carolina and Tennessee from the 1800s until the coming of the railroad.

Drovers road horseback along this former Indian path, in front of immense numbers of cattle and hogs that were driven through the river valley for sale to seaboard markets. There was even an annual turkey drive, where thousands of the gobblers made way to upstate South Carolina for their ultimate date with a slaughterhouse. Tavern-keepers with hog stands set up shop along the turnpike, where they sometimes fed up to 100,000 hogs in a single day.

The Woodfin to Hot Springs stretch of river featured stands at Alexander, Marshall, Barnard, and Stackhouse, offering the weary farmer respite in the form of poker and alcohol, together with the opportunity to fraternize with sometimes "shady" characters. The Civil War suspended railroad construction and thereby prolonged the utility of this rudimentary form of interstate commerce, but the rails were joined with their western link in 1882 at the Tennessee line. At that point it is said that the turnpike traffic ceased about as abruptly as it began.

Returning to Walnut Island Park, the voyage to the mouth of the Ivy River is slightly less than 5 miles and represents "home court" to the author, having traversed this riverway well over a hundred times. Each time, however, fosters a unique experience all its own. As noted by Heraclius (540-480 B.C.), one "cannot step twice into the same river; for other waters are ever flowing on to you." Great blue heron and Canada geese frequently join us on this section, together with the occasional otter, beaver, or white-tailed deer.

After a small rapid next to the park, the river is calm for about a half-mile with Sandy Mush Creek entering on the left. Paddle under the railroad trestle and stop for a drink while listening to the rushing water. Continue on and you cross into Madison County in less than a mile. The river makes a horseshoe turn at Bailey Bend (locals call it *"turkey neck curve"*), named for the family of former Madison Sheriff Jesse James Bailey. Sheriff Bailey was in office during the time of prohibition, and waged a war on moonshiners that later became known as the era of Bloody Madison.

Rock outcroppings with sheer faces appear on river right across from Mussell Shell Island, which are fondly known to some as Mariah's Lookout, Dylan's Ledge, and Falling Rock Gap (yes, we named the island also). Moderate Class I-II whitewater, interspersed with stretches of flatwater, is the rule until you reach Panhandle Shoals, about 2 miles from Bailey Bend. If the river is high, it would be advisable to scout this area of rock garden, which is the only significant segment of white-water during the run. The Ivy appears on your right about a mile from Panhandle, and an easy take-out on 251 is about 50 yards upstream of the confluence.

As an alternative, you can choose to continue on to the county access at the community of Rollins (approximately another 2 miles), or take out just prior to the 8' Capitola Dam in Marshall about a mile from Rollins. Marshall, formerly known as Lapland, is the county seat of Madison with river on one side and mountain on the other. As noted by Wilma Dykeman, folks know it as the town that is "a block wide, a mile long, sky high and hell deep." Biennerhassett Island sits in the middle of the river just next to downtown, and can serve as a put-in for a 2 mile moving water run to the 25' Redmon Dam if you so desire. From Redmon to Barnard, a trip of about 5.5 miles, consistent Class II whitewater takes you into forested wilderness and away from the highway.

Rafting expeditions rule the downstream section from Barnard to Stackhouse to Hot Springs, which is not recommended for open boaters or novice paddlers. This run of about 9 miles through Pisgah National Forest, does, however, offer some of the most remote river wilderness in western North Carolina. If you accept the challenge, a ghost town known as Runion awaits your exploration at the mouth of Big Laurel Creek.

Also accessible via the Big Laurel hiking trail just off 25/70, Runion was a logging camp village of approximately a thousand people at the turn of the 20th Century. Stone foundations nestled within the temperate rainforest jungle are all that remain of the once bustling community. Hot Springs awaits about 3 miles downstream, and be sure to take a soak in the natural thermal spa waters while in the area. The Nantahala Outdoor Center maintains a parking area for river access in this town of about 500 residents, and the open boater can enjoy the option of returning to the water here.

Formerly known as Warm Springs, the town served as headquarters for the Confederate Provisional Forces under General Davis during the Civil War, but was taken by federal troops in 1863. Earlier that same year, the cruelty of the war had reached a dark pinnacle when a Confederate lieutenant colonel authorized the firing squad execution of what were thought to be Union sympathizers, one a mere 14 years of age. Known as the Shelton

Laurel Massacre, the manhunt was in response to a series of break-ins that had occurred the previous month in Marshall. Only food and necessary supplies had been stolen, and some of the helpless captives had not even been part of the raid. Such was not a time for due process.

If you choose to put-in amid the take-out of rafts at Hot Springs, save an hour or so to hike up the Silvermine Trail to Lover's Leap, where it joins the Appalachian Trail (the route of the latter, running from Georgia to its northern terminus in Maine, treks right through downtown Hot Springs). The trail head is only a short walk from the Nantahala access, and the kids might just see a glint of silver from the long-lost mine along the way. Treasure hunters have searched for the entrance to the mine for many years, but to no avail. A panoramic river vista awaits at Lover's Leap, where, like many other spots found at various North American river valleys, an Indian maiden supposedly jumped after learning that her betrothed would not be coming back to her.

Shortly after you hit the river, on river-left you will see the spa grounds and foundational structures from days gone by when Hot Springs was a booming resort. The grounds even served as a German prisoner-of-war camp during World War I, and the detainees actually built cabins with intricate carpentry detail during their tenure of encampment. The river here is active but manageable for a family venture with reasonable caution. Paint Creek Road runs along the eastern edge, but soon turns to dirt/gravel after leaving town. Not a bad bicycle shuttle if you are up for it. Only a few homes can be seen in the distance off shore as the river continues to bisect Pisgah National Forest.

Murray Branch river access is about 4 miles down-stream, and you will reach Paint Rock after another 2.5 miles. Named for the Native American drawings that formerly adorned it, the rock formation stands tall as a remaining colonial boundary between North Carolina and Tennessee. In 1793, early settlers erected a block-house fortress here in an effort to provide protection from Indian attacks, and such appears on many maps from the pioneer era. At this point, Paint Creek enters the French Broad on river-right and Pisgah gives way to Cherokee National Forest.

The French Broad, *the Long Man,* or *Acguiqua,* now leaves us behind as it continues its journey to the Mississippi. Soon nothing will be left of *Tahkeyostee* wild water, and the gorge will eventually give way to farmland reminiscent of that found in the river headwaters. In fact, the river will soon settle into the 32,000 acre TVA impoundment known as Lake Douglas located just the other side of Newport. It survives the spillway and winds through eastern Tennessee until joining with the Holston River just before entering the Knoxville area. Viola, the Tennessee River is born!

We are thankful for the river who has graced Western North Carolina with its presence for centuries; the river who, according to the Cherokee, rests its head on the mountains with its feet along the valleys, being fed by its chattering children; the river of our family during our time, and the river that waits for you and yours.

Carrot Island, Beaufort. Look close and you may find a
wild Mustang.

Hammock House, Beaufort. An 18th century pirate refuge.

William D. Auman

From the late 1990s: Dylan at Plum Point, Bath.
Former site of Blackbeard's civilian home.

The Elizabeth II, Shallowbag Bay, Manteo.

A lazy 'gator at Lake Waccamaw

Cypress dugout canoe on display at Halifax

The author on the Cape Fear River, circa 1985.

Mariah at the helm, approaching the Cliffs of the Neuse, circa 2002.

Inside Boone's Cave along the Yadkin

An Indian village on the Uwharrie River?
(actually a Boy Scout Camp)

William D. Auman

Poplar dugout on display at the Catawba Indian Reservation.

Lake Glenville

View of the Biltmore House from the French Broad River

Who says we need canoe racks?

Along the New River

Poplar dugout displayed at the Cherokee Indian Reservation

Liz at the helm on Lake Santeelah.

The author at Fontana Lake, circa 1998.

William D. Auman

Paint Rock

Mariah and Dylan about to embark, 1995.

Chapter Four:

About the "Younglings" and Safety

As renowned canoeist Bill Riviere once commented, "paddling will never be as safe as going to prayer meeting." People do lose their lives every year, but I've never known a canoe or kayak to flip on its own accord. There will always be those who attempt to tackle rapids that are beyond their capabilities, or those who fail to take adequate precautions during the seemingly routine excursion.

Common sense, caution, and practicality account for 99% of safe passage, but it doesn't hurt to be aware of a few rules of thumb. First, make certain at least one adult in your entourage is a competent swimmer, and ensure that ALL parties wear an appropriate personal flotation device at all times when on the water. Second, be aware of river hazards and avoid them, i.e. high water, strainers, and cold. When the water and air temperatures are less than a combined 100 degrees Fahrenheit, a wet-suit should be worn. Finally, beware of weirs and souse holes where the river drops over an obstacle, then curls back into a stationary wave. When this occurs, surface water is actually going upstream and trapping any object caught between the drop and the wave. Once trapped, a swimmer's only hope is to dive below the surface or try to swim out from the end of the wave.

You should always be aware of the difficulty classi-fication that could be encountered during your journey. This book is devoted to the family "wilderness" experi-ence, and therefore generally focuses on no higher than Class I or II whitewater. A few sections may include some Class III segments, which feature rapids with high, irregular waves that are capable of swamping a canoe, together with narrow passages that may require scouting. I have attempted to point out those within that potential class, but remember that high water levels can cause a class to be upgraded. Only the extremely experienced boater should attempt Class IV or V, with Class VI reserved for the expert who will at some point be fea-tured on ESPN's extreme sports special series (assuming they survive the descent).

In case of upset, try to hold on to your boat and get to the upstream end so that you will not be pinned against upcoming obstacles. Keep your feet near the sur-face and pointed downstream, and make sure you get to slow or very shallow water before attempting to stand.

Some say never to paddle alone, but there is nothing like a subjective "Zen in the moment" experience that is unique to the individual paddler. Although probably good advice from a safety standpoint, I would temper that with the same application of common sense to be utilized during a voyage of any number. If you go alone, be prepared and responsible, and make certain that someone who is likewise responsible is aware of your itinerary. In the event of capsize or other mishap, it would be comforting to know that someone will soon be calling 911 on your behalf. Remember that caution and prevention are critical themes, and any judgment calls should be made with a healthy sense of conservatism.

A "survival kit" is always a good idea, even for the hour-long adventure. Invest in a small dry-bag, or make your own out of a heavy duty trash bag or tackle box. Include matches, a whistle, knife, mirror, compass, small flashlight, space blanket, candle, and a couple of energy or candy bars. If on a coastal paddle, be sure not to forget the pint of rum (that will help get you through the ordeal in case you forgot the cell phone).

Last but not least, the children! Needless to say, it caused quite a stir among many when it became known that our son hit the water at age three *(see the upcoming story in Part Five),* not to mention the even greater shock of our daughter starting at two. On another occasion, I fondly remember my Aunt's incredulous look when I answered "yes, I have taken them canoeing within a stone's throw of alligators." Was I a bad parent? Well, none of us are perfect, but I think if you ask either of our young adults if paddling while toddling was a negative, a resounding "Not at all" would be their response.

I'd like to think that we exposed them to a world of discovery and love of nature, together with their history-buff father's penchant for colonial era engagement. Any age is a good age to begin, and it's not difficult to plan an excursion that will serve as a basis for lifetime memories. A twelve year-old may not enjoy a dinosaur hunt, but perhaps a scavenger hunt for arrowheads would suffice on that mountain sandbar. If at the coast, there's always pirate treasure, shark teeth, shells and sand dollars to look for.

Your budding ecologist might wish to keep a check-list on the number of birds, ducks, geese, raptors, or sunning 'gators that you encounter. There will likely be deer, raccoon, or other animal tracks to investigate along the shoreline. Your little leaguer will enjoy the challenge of target practice using the bucket of rocks that you brought along for he or she to throw. If it's warm, there is nothing like a swim through gentle rapids or a paddle-splashing contest.

These are but a few ideas among many. The beauty of the family experience is that you make it your own. Treasured memories are ready and waiting for you to create. Don't let any peculiar fears stand in the way of that. As noted by the late Pierre Pulling, aboriginal paddlers adhered to a fundamental safety code. First, they used good judgment. Before they acquired this judgment they depended upon someone else who had it. Second, they rarely allowed themselves to get into a dangerous situation. If, in spite of precautions, a dangerous situation developed, they generally had developed the skill to paddle out of it. Those time-honored standards continue to serve the contemporary paddler, so get out there and hit the water.

Dylan is ready to dinosaur hunt, 1991

Chapter Five:

Searching for Dinosaurs by canoe

In keeping within the "family wilderness" theme which has consistently surfaced throughout this book, I have included the following article which was originally written back in 1992, and was first published by what was then known as the *Greenline* magazine. The *Greenline* has subsequently evolved into Asheville's *Mountain Express*, a weekly publication that features a variety of entertainment and outdoor articles, in addition to providing a guidebook for the local arts, theaters, clubs, and restaurants. This article speaks of but one of the many paddling adventures that we have been fortunate to experience throughout the years. I hope you enjoy reading it as much as I did writing it, and living it.

"Daddy, look—it's a flying dinosaur!" I almost dropped our Old Town Pathfinder while removing it from the car rack, trying to see just what creature my three-year old son Dylan was referring to. In the nick of time, I caught a fleeting glimpse of two Canada geese making their way across the cove on the southern tip of Lake Keowee (okay, so we're now in South Carolina, but the book title does include the designation of "Carolina"). Before I had a chance to explain to my son that, no, they were not pterodactyls, additional members of the flock decided to join us on the banks of the peninsula where we intended to camp.

Dylan immediately dropped the stick he was using as his "Peter Pan sword" in defense of the squirrels at the campground, and ran to get a closer look. The first honk made him hesitate, but soon a goose was eating bread right out of his hand. Who said a February canoe-camping trip with a pre-schooler was a bad idea?

This was our first overnighter as a twosome. Needless to say, it would be a test for both of us. But this was our time to watch the ripples of wind on the water, to look for arrowheads, throw rocks, and, of course, to venture forth by boat in search of dinosaurs and other wildlife. Accordingly, the three of us (we couldn't forget Captain Planet) launched the canoe and left behind the sated geese, who seemed content to watch our journey from shore.

We couldn't have picked a better time. No offense to the Minnesota loyalists of the Boundary Waters Canoe Area, but Western North Carolinians have our own boundary waters to explore. Lake Keowee is the larger of two adjoining lakes (Jocassee is the other) in upstate South Carolina, just off Cherokee Scenic Highway 11. To the north, the Appalachians provide a mountainous backdrop as they retreat into the Old North State. With over 225 miles of shoreline, Keowee is naturally popular with sailors and power boaters, but in two days of paddling we saw only a handful of either.

"Daddy, I want to go over there." This time it was the rocky shore of a small island filled with sweet smelling Carolina pines. Before that, it was a sandy beach near the county park where we camped. How this child maintains the stamina necessary to support his sense of adventure, I'll never know. Maybe the raccoon tracks on the soft sand, obviously made by Ninja Turtles in disguise, en route to their secret hideaway deep in the forest, had something to do with it.

We did eventually make it back to camp, and spent the remainder of the evening around the fire telling stories about the brave Indian boys (Dylan's age, of course), who used to inhabit the region. The Keowee area was once part of the Cherokee Nation, but the tribe was forced to evacuate the vicinity somewhere in the neighborhood of 1776. They subsequently lost their land after being defeated by the South Carolina militia near the end of the Revolutionary War, though many descendants of those who avoided the Trail of Tears still live on the reservation about an hour north.

When morning came, Dylan spotted a sea gull, presumably attempting a return to Myrtle Beach? A sea gull five hours from the Atlantic? In February? Surprising to say the least, but the fact that our son brought it to my attention was no longer a surprise. Thoreau once said that nature bears the close inspection of an insect's eye view, and Dylan practices that precept constantly. His eyes are level with the detail of all that is new and exciting, his imagination creating a degree of perception all its own.

Even when scattered showers came our way, the child's spirit (which by now had rubbed off on me) overcame any disappointment. The hardest thing was having to say no when Dylan wanted to pitch the tent in our backyard upon our return home. My clothes were saturated enough by then, but they'll be a next time soon.

All of you paddlers with small children can enhance your own enjoyment by including them in your journeys. Their sense of inquiry and wonder can bring a refreshing perspective to your life as a canoeist or kayaker. Once a child has conquered the fear of water and will obediently sit in a stationary position, he or she is ready for a maiden voyage. With reasonable caution and personal flotation devices, your possibilities are unlimited. Dylan was initiated at age 2, and now can assist with his own 30-inch paddle. Our one year-old daughter already wants to join us. Her time will soon arrive.

POSTSCRIPT

The late Jimmy Valvano, former North Carolina State basketball coach and an inspiration to the author and countless others, once said that to fully experience each day one needs to laugh, cry, and think. I would add, if possible...go paddling. The quote from legendary canoeist and author Sigurd Olson is worthy of repeat, for "a man is part of his canoe and therefore part of all he knows. The instant he dips a paddle, he flows as it flows, the canoe yielding to his slightest touch, responsive to his every whim and thought. The paddle is an extension of his arm as his arm is a part of his body. Should you be lucky enough to be moving across a calm surface with mirrored clouds, you may have the sensation of suspension between heaven and earth, of paddling not on water but through the skies themselves." A beautiful description, yet the experience cannot be accessed through the written word alone. Your journey awaits.

Acknowledgements

My thanks go out to all who have encouraged and supported this endeavor, many of whom may have simply shared a paddling experience or offered a positive word of suggestion. Others who have played a larger role must be noted: Elizabeth, my wife and paddling partner, who has always insisted that I had "water on the brain"; Dylan, our son who always notices the intricacies of nature that others often miss; Mariah, our daughter who has evolved into perhaps the most kindred of paddling spirits; Jamal Mullen and David Belser, my exceptionally talented friends and editorial consultants ; and, last, but not least, Carolyn and David, my parents who are responsible for that 1973 Christmas surprise...the author's first boat, without which a lifetime of paddling may possibly have been missed.

INDEX TO REFERENCED BODIES OF WATER

(*note: references organized pursuant to initial mention in text, some entries are discussed in more than one chapter)

A. Chapter One

B. Chapter Two

Recommended Reading &
Select Resources

American Red Cross

Benner, Bob, Carolina Whitewater (Menasha Ridge
    Press, Birmingham, 1981)

Coastal Wildlife Refuge Society, Manteo, North Car-
    olina

Day, Jean, Carolina Indians (Golden Age, 1998)

Dykeman, Wilma, The French Broad (University of Ten-
    nessee Press, 1955)

Faragher, John Mack, Daniel Boone (Holt, 1992)

Land of Sky Regional Council (Asheville)

Lawrence, Bill, The Early American Wilderness (Paragon House, 1991)

North Carolina Department of Commerce, Division of Tourism

North Carolina Department of Environment and Natural Resources

North Carolina Wildlife Resources Commission

Pulling, Pierre, Canoeing the Indian Way (Stackpole, 1979)

Riverlink of Asheville, North Carolina

Riviere, Bill, The Open Canoe (Little, Brown & Co., 1985)

Roberts, Nancy, Blackbeard & Other Pirates of the Atlantic Coast (Bair, 1993)

Tellico Plains (TN) Mountain Press

United States Forest Service

Wooden Canoe Heritage Association

LaVergne, TN USA
07 February 2011
215620LV00001B/2/P

9 781608 445264